Accelerating Company Growth is a brief and to-the-point [guide to] constructing a growth plan for your business. It's filled with concrete and succinct stories that provide practical advice and encouragement for the aspiring entrepreneur. **Sean O'Sullivan, Founder, SOSventures International**

Brendan has done a great job here in illustrating the importance of leadership and providing guidelines on how to become a great leader – we can all learn from this and we should all strive to be better. **Peter Hiscocks, CEO, Executive Education, Cambridge Judge Business School**

Accelerating Company Growth is a real page-turner: a compelling and inspiring introduction to the complex field of SME acceleration. Brendan Dowling engagingly combines anecdote and analysis in refracting through the sympathetic lens of his own varied experience much of the research into successful entrepreneurship of the past dozen years. Key concepts from the elevator pitch to the value proposition are succinctly explained through examples that fit together in a clear, modular way. Jargon is judiciously deployed where it illuminates central concepts entrepreneurs are likely to encounter negotiating with investors (business model, red ocean), and considerable emphasis is rightly placed on sales and marketing. Above all, the author never loses sight of the human motivation and social potential of growth entrepreneurship. I read it on a long flight and didn't notice the hours roll by. A book I wish I'd encountered years ago. **David Gill, Managing Director, St John's Innovation Centre, Cambridge**

Brendan's book is a welcome addition to the subject of accelerating business growth. The richness of his own experience provides great credibility and also gives very practical information that will motivate those who are on this path. It is also a compelling read! **Siobhan McAleer, Commercial Director, Irish Management Institute**

The book offers hard-earned and valuable advice to entrepreneurs on issues that they and their companies will face on a rapid growth trajectory. It is accessible and short – and repeated reading will reveal its many nuggets of wisdom. **Joey Mason, Partner, Delta Partners**

Brendan possesses that unique 'can do' attitude that is prevalent in genuine entrepreneurs. Having worked with him on a number of major projects, I can attest to his 'practice what you preach' business approach. This book is an honest representation of the challenges that face most SMEs as they strive for accelerated growth and many CEOs will readily identify and relate to Brendan's experiences. **Ian Sparling, CEO, Soft-ex Communications**

This is a comprehensive book that includes all the elements to building a robust plan for accelerating growth. It is very practical and written from Brendan's wide experience rather than an academic perspective. **Paul O'Dea, CEO, Select Strategies**

A very easy-to-read approach, with an easy-to-use framework, for CEOs wanting to understand the key elements involved in accelerating the growth of their business. Brendan has first-hand experience and is a natural storyteller. **Mary Goulding, Strategic Business Coach to CEOs**

Brendan Dowling speaks from a deep well of experience, having started and managed a string of successful enterprises. In this compelling book, he relays his experiences and speaks from the heart about success – and failure – in business, with myriad tips and techniques for accelerating growth. Highly recommended. **Dermot Duff, Executive Learning Director, Irish Management Institute & Associate Professor, Trinity College Dublin Business School**

People who manage growing businesses are among the busiest around. They don't have time to read many books, but they should read this one. Brendan Dowling has distilled many really valuable insights from his varied and successful entrepreneurial career. The advice he offers on how to grow a business is supported throughout by examples from his own experience. The book is not only a pleasure to read, but is structured in a way that makes it a valuable reference work as key growth challenges arise. **Dr John McMackin, Director of Executive and International Education, Dublin City University Business School**

ACCELERATING COMPANY GROWTH

A Practical Guide for CEOs

Brendan Dowling

Published by OAK TREE PRESS, 19 Rutland Street, Cork, Ireland

www.oaktreepress.com

© 2014 Brendan Dowling

A catalogue record of this book is available from the British Library.

ISBN 978 1 78119 111 8 (paperback)
ISBN 978 1 78119 112 5 (ePub)
ISBN 978 1 78119 113 2 (Kindle)

Cover design: Kieran O'Connor Design
Cover illustration: Rick Tomlinson / Volvo Ocean Race
Author photo: Robert Redmond Studios

All rights reserved. No part of this publication may be reproduced or transmitted in any form or by any means, including photocopying and recording, without written permission of the publisher. Such written permission must also be obtained before any part of this publication is stored in a retrieval system of any nature. Requests for permission should be directed to Oak Tree Press, 19 Rutland Street, Cork, Ireland or info@oaktreepress.com.

The information contained in this publication is intended for guideline purposes only and does not represent legal advice. Readers should always seek independent legal and/or other professional advice specific to their own requirements before taking any action based on the information provided herein.

CONTENTS

	MyGoodPoints.com	v
	Dedication	vi
	Acknowledgements	vii
	Introduction	1
1	Creating Your Accelerated Growth Plan	3

Section 1: The Pre-requisites for Accelerated Growth

2	Motivation	9
3	Leadership	17
4	Vision	25
5	Strategy	31

Section 2: The Components of Accelerated Growth

6	Summarizing What You Do in an Elevator Pitch	39
7	Communicating Your Value Proposition to Your Customers	47
8	Sizing the Market Opportunity	59
9	What Problem Do You Solve for Your Customers?	69
10	Communicating Your Message to the Market	77
11	Achieving Your Sales Targets	85
12	How Do You Make Money?	99
13	How Do You Beat the Competition?	105
14	You Need a Great Team	113
15	Funding Accelerated Growth	123
16	Managing the Business	129

Section 3: Other Contributors to Accelerated Growth

17	Making Best Use of Your Board of Directors	139
18	Working with Venture Capitalists	147
19	Selling Your Company	157
20	Behaving Ethically in Business	171

Conclusion   179

Appendices

1	Accelerated Growth Plan Slide Deck Template	181
2	Accelerated Growth Plan Sample Slide Deck: Nautique2	189
3	Further Reading	198

About the Author   199

mygoodpoints.com
people power for good

All author proceeds from ACCELERATING COMPANY GROWTH will be donated to the MyGoodPoints.com charity.

MyGoodPoints.com is a new online charity that is harnessing the power of technology, people and corporate CSR, combined with business principles, to revolutionize the charity sector. MyGoodPoints will change how people engage with charities by providing a single online charity account, through which a donor can collect funds using loyalty points, payroll deductions, tax back and online payments, then donate these funds to any charity of their choice and receive multimedia feedback from the charity workers to see where the funds have been applied.

MyGoodPoints' objective is to reverse the downward trend in giving by creating the next generation of donors by:

- **Changing people's behavior:** The number of donors and the volume of donations is falling; we want to create a culture of giving, focused on youth, by making it free to give (loyalty points), giving fantastic feedback and accountability and by making it cool and fun to be a donor on MyGoodPoints;

- **Aligning objectives:** By aligning the objectives of donors, large corporates, charities and recipients, we can harness the power of people around a common purpose. Donors will benefit from giving and responsible corporates want customer loyalty, charities want more funding and recipients need help;

- **Driving efficiencies in charities:** Charities on MyGoodPoints will need to compete with each other to attract the donor's funds; this will drive more accountability and better feedback to donors and ultimately drive efficiencies through donor scrutiny.

For more information, visit **www.mygoodpoints.com**.

DEDICATION

To my wife (my business coach) and four amazing children, who have been so patient and supportive while I worked away on this book.

ACKNOWLEDGEMENTS

For the front cover of this book I chose the image of a racing yacht in full sail, capturing the power of the wind and crashing through waves, as it accelerates through the blue ocean (*the* place for all great companies), because to me this is the best representation of what it is like to accelerate company growth. To go this fast you need to have a great team who know what they are doing and who work in perfect harmony, under the leadership of a great captain, who makes the right decisions on what direction to go and the sails to use for the wind conditions, currents, waves and all the other elements that are thrown at you by the unpredictable environment. It can be a rough ride and sometimes you can take on water, to the point of thinking that you may sink, but when you get everything right the excitement and adrenalin rush that comes from the acceleration, as you ride and crash through waves under your own power, is invigorating – just like accelerating the growth of your company.

I would like to thank Volvo Ocean Race (**www.volvooceanrace.com**) – as soon as I explained what this book was about, they understood what I was trying to convey and agreed to provide this image, royalty-free for use on the cover.

I also would like to thank the many people who helped create and shape this book through their comments and advice. In particular, Karl Aherne, Fr Paddy Carbery, John Colgan, Dermot Duff, Jerry Ennis, Charles Garvey, David Gill, Mary Goulding, Peter Hiscocks, Mary Kinnane, Joey Mason, Siobhan McAleer, John McMackin, Sean Melly, Denis Murphy, Paul O'Dea, Sean O'Sullivan, Sean Prior, Ian Sparling and Aidan Stack, as well all the many entrepreneurs I have had the pleasure of working with during my career.

INTRODUCTION

I have owned and operated many different businesses over the past 20 years – how time flies when you are having fun! For the most part, it has been great fun, but starting and growing your own business is not for the faint-hearted.

I started my business career when I was in college, trading on the streets of Irish towns and over the years I have worked my way up to operating in the boardrooms of international companies. I have had a number of spectacular successes and some spectacular failures – and I have learned a lot from both.

I have been privileged to receive great academic education, but my drive for education was sparked by witnessing my father's business fail when I was a teenager. He had built up a number of successful businesses, but a single significant change in market circumstances beyond his control brought him down. This gave me the drive and determination to have a qualification that I could fall back on if my business ever went bust. I am glad I did get my qualifications (Commerce degree, MBA, Chartered Accountant and Executive Coach), because sometimes I have needed to get consulting roles, between companies, or at times when my own company could not pay me a salary, which has been too often for my liking.

So I have learned about starting and growing a business both from the classroom and by doing it in the field. Needless to say the most intense learning happens in the field and not in the classroom. On a recent executive training program where I participated as a speaker and coach, the CEOs attending repeatedly stated that it was a story from an experienced business leader that inspired them to change direction or to accelerate their company's growth through implementing the learning.

It is this first-hand experience that has inspired me to write this book. I want to provide you with practical experience that can be implemented in your business to help you to accelerate its growth. I will not give you any classroom theory, only practical advice that I have learned in the field or taken from other colleagues who eat, live and breathe business growth in the real world. This book contains stories and tips that are based on practical experience, learned while growing companies.

One of my overriding reasons for writing this book was the fact that I received very little practical advice myself as I started and grew my own businesses. I did not have a mentor or coach and practical books with real business advice were hard to come by. I wish I had these resources myself when I started out on the journey for the first time.

I often equate reading an academic-based business book to reading the manual of your new cell phone: you know you will learn a lot and get more out of your phone if you read it carefully but, if you are like me, you find the book too boring to read, and so you struggle on until you get some practical tips from other users. I have tried to make this book interesting – a 'good read,' not a manual – with stories and tips to help you in accelerating your company's growth from someone who has been there and done that. In effect, these are the short cuts to getting the most from your business.

I sincerely hope that you enjoy reading this book and that you take a lot from it, and that it helps you to grow your business beyond what you would have achieved on your own.

Please note that throughout this book I have used real-life stories and examples based on my own business experiences, but I have changed names and places to protect the identity of the people involved and exaggerated certain stories to make a point. Nonetheless, the basis of all the stories is true and the changes are not critical to the learning.

Brendan Dowling
October 2013

1
CREATING YOUR ACCELERATED GROWTH PLAN

Throughout this book I have set out to give you practical advice and stories, based on my own experience, which will help you to accelerate the growth of your business. In addition in **Appendix 1** I have included a slide deck template that you can use to form the basis of your own Accelerated Growth Plan. Gone are the days of creating several hundred page-long business plans to be read by all the stakeholders in the business; today, people prefer to summarize the key points of a growth plan or an investor pitch in a dozen or so slides that provide the big picture with the details, such as market research, product specifications, financial model, etc. available on demand elsewhere. As you read through the key areas that need to be covered in all good Accelerated Growth Plans in the following chapters, I will refer to the slide that summarizes the area just covered and give you some tips to help you to complete your own version.

First in **Section 1** I cover the pre-requisites for accelerating company growth: motivation, leadership, vision and strategy. Unless you get these right, none of the other drivers of growth covered in **Section 2** will matter very much.

In **Section 2** I cover the key areas that drive company growth, giving you advice and tips from my own experience: your elevator pitch; value proposition; market; the customer's problem and your solution; marketing; sales; business model; competitors; team/people; finances; and operations.

At the end of each of these chapters, I will show you how to complete a slide for your Accelerated Growth Plan that covers all the points critical to having a document that forms the blueprint for your company's growth.

When developing your own slide deck, keep it to 10 to 12 slides, certainly no more than 15. Use as few words as possible in a large font with pictures and illustrations to help the reader to take it all in quickly. Your Accelerated Growth Plan should be simple and punchy and to make it relevant to different audiences – your board, senior management team, employees, customers, banks, suppliers – use different selections of the slides for different audiences.

Once you have planned each aspect of your Accelerated Growth Plan sufficiently, summarize it on the appropriate slide. But keep your underlying research, findings, calculations, decisions, etc. on hand to answer queries.

Making your slide deck as short and punchy as possible will take time. For example, it took me the best part of three years to define my latest product offering as:

> **Customer Relationship Engagement (CRE),** which allows an enterprise to engage its customers in two-way communications that are targeted, personalized and permission-based.

I went through a lot of mumbo-jumbo before I got to this wording, but I kept working at it, trying versions that did not quite convey the right message. At one stage I awakened unwanted competition when I used the term 'customer relationship management' (CRM). I was always looking for feedback, and trying to break away from a crowded market to find a new 'blue ocean' that we could dominate as a small start-up. Although this takes time to get right, when you achieve it the words will sound so natural, they will become part of the language of everyone in your organization and beyond (your customers, suppliers, investors, etc.). Keep going back to the words you use and the conclusions you make until they are so concise and understandable that everyone is perfectly clear about what you are trying to convey.

And finally in **Section 3** I look at some other topics that are important contributors to accelerated company growth: how to use your board of directors; working with venture capital funding; selling your company (the end-game for most of us); and, dear to my own heart, business ethics.

The steps and components needed to develop an Accelerated Growth Plan and slide deck for your own business are:

- Start by establishing some credibility: who you are, what you have done to date, your customers, etc. (**Chapter 6: Summarizing What You Do in an Elevator Pitch**);
- Then talk about what you do: make sure that your audience knows exactly what your business does before you go on (**Chapter 7: Communicating Your Value Proposition to Your Customers**);
- Describe the scale of the market opportunity (**Chapter 8: Sizing the Market Opportunity**);
- Explain the problem that exists in the market and how you solve it (**Chapter 9: What Problem Do You Solve for Your Customers?**);

- Show how you will reach this market (**Chapter 10: Communicating Your Message to the Market** and **Chapter 11: Achieving Your Sales Targets**);
- Explain how you will make money (**Chapter 12: How Do You Make Money?**);
- Explain how you can win against competitors (**Chapter 13: How Do You Beat the Competition?**);
- Talk about the great people that are on board or soon to be recruited (**Chapter 14: You Need a Great Team**);
- Show how much money can be made and how you plan to fund this growth (**Chapter 15: Funding Accelerated Growth**);
- Show how you can deliver the business and manage it (**Chapter 16: Managing the Business**).

To show you what I mean, in **Appendix 2** I provide a sample slide deck for a fictitious company, Nautique2 – based on my first business, Nautique, as if I were starting it again from scratch today.

The more you can present your Accelerated Growth Plan as a story about your business, the easier it will be to remember and to communicate and the better it will be in convincing other stakeholders to come on your journey and to help you to accelerate your company's growth and, ultimately, to achieve greater success for your business.

SECTION 1

THE PRE-REQUISITES FOR ACCELERATED GROWTH

2
MOTIVATION

- Why did you create the business and why do you want to accelerate its growth?
- Achieving a goal
- Work/life balance and the price of success
- Manage the risks
- You can do it if you believe you can
- Learn to believe in yourself
- Making a difference
- Be passionate about what you do

Motivation is important because ...

Accelerating the growth of a business is not for the faint-hearted. There is huge commitment, sacrifice and risks involved and the outcome is unknown (you could win – or you could lose). Motivation is the foundation on which all successful business acceleration is based; if you don't have the level of motivation needed, then it will be very difficult to drive for growth.

If you don't have the motivation to grow your business, or it is waning a little, take on a business coach. They can help you to take a deep look at yourself and your business and try to understand what makes you tick and what drives you – what's important to you and what you want to achieve and why.

The poet Henry Wadsworth Longfellow (1807 – 1882) put it best:

> The heights by great men reached and kept
> Were not attained by sudden flight
> But they, while their companions slept,
> Were toiling upward in the night.

I don't think much has changed since then in terms of the motivation needed to succeed.

Why did you create the business and why do you want to accelerate its growth?

You need to answer these two questions before you set out to accelerate the growth of your business.

One of my ventures (**www.MyGoodPoints.com**) is a not-for-profit charity. I am passionate about it and determined to revolutionize the global charity sector, by using the latest technologies and by aligning the objectives of large corporations through their CSR strategy, to motivate people and corporations to change the world by participating and becoming active donors. I have put a lot of my own time and money into this venture, time that is very scarce and money that is even scarcer in the current environment. Recently someone who I admire and respect asked me why I was doing this instead of concentrating only on my for-profit venture. My immediate and natural response was simply "Because I can." Often entrepreneurs drive for growth simply because they can – they have great products and people that allow them to be a global success.

Some people are motivated purely by money but as much as getting cash out is a key measure of success, it is not always the key driver for success. In my experience, the greatest leaders of highly successful companies are motivated by a vision and passion for what they can achieve, not how much money they can make. The one venture that I created purely to make a lot of money was a plant hire business that I started after seeing a friend of mine make a lot of money from his own plant hire business. Hire Store failed, costing me a lot of money that I did not have. It was a hard lesson, but I am convinced that the reason it failed was that my motivation was not at the same level as in my other businesses where I was passionate about what I was doing, enjoyed the work, etc.

For me, a key motivation always has been the sense of challenge. I love a challenge and all my life I have challenged the way things are or should be with my own view of the way they could be and will be. This got me into a lot of trouble in school and college. I believe that great leaders in business have a burning passion and vision of how the world *can be* with their products or services changing the way things were. Steve Jobs of Apple epitomized this. Although several years ago I created a venture called Digital Versatile Media that offered digital content services on PC and cell phones in a similar way to how Apple iTunes does it today, what we had was good but not good enough. We did well and I am sure that, if we had stuck to our core strategy, we would have been successful. But I am also sure that we could never have achieved the levels of success achieved by Steve Jobs. If you read his life story, you will know why. As much drive and determination as I have, I don't come close to what Steve Jobs had.

Achieving a goal

There is also a huge sense of pride in achieving a goal in business – in creating a new product that eventually sits on the same shelf as a competing and established product and outsells them.

My first venture was a premium aftershave company called Nautique. My key competitor was Polo (Ralph Lauren). To get my product on the same shelf as Polo aftershave, in the top cosmetic retail store in Ireland (Brown Thomas), was a huge achievement that gave me an enormous sense of satisfaction, but to outsell Polo in our first year of trading by many times gave me an even greater sense of achievement.

When you observe top sports people, the sheer passion, drive and determination that they have for their sport is frightening; they are so focused and hardworking, almost to the exclusion of everything else in their lives. It is this type of determination that motivates a CEO to accelerate the growth of their company beyond what others would accept as good enough.

We have moved on from a world where our motivations were driven mainly by the basic needs for food and shelter. Dan Pink, in his book *Drive*, argues that, if you allow someone to master their skills, this is by far a greater motivator than money or titles. Mastering is where motivation is at today.

Work / life balance and the price of success

Our work and our business achievements are a huge part of who and what we are as entrepreneurs. We try to get the work / life balance right and many of us in business today would love to have more time and money to spend more time with our family and friends.

But I also know people who achieved the huge 'exit' and have millions sitting in the bank. Most of them took a year or two out of the business fast lane but then threw themselves back into the thick of it with a new venture.

It is who we entrepreneurs are and I believe that, to have a happy and fulfilled life, we need our work as a balance to our personal lives.

There are huge sacrifices to be made if you want to really accelerate the growth of your business. You are in the office day and night; you are always on the phone when you are at home; you are always travelling; you miss all the children's events and even when you are there you are not present (as my mother says about me).

In one of my ventures, we were selling to mobile operators and content providers all over the world from our offices in London and New York. I commuted from Ireland to the London office every week and to New York monthly, but once I got to London, often I was straight onto another plane to countries like India, Pakistan, Vietnam, Malaysia, Kenya, Ghana or Singapore. Typically, I flew to a country overnight, sleeping on the plane, did the meeting, sometimes catching a little sleep in a hotel room before flying back to London again. I remember one trip where I did my usual commute to London and then tried to board a British Airways flight to Vietnam but when I went to the check-in desk they could not check me in. After a number of different supervisors had tried to solve the problem, the duty manager was called. He asked, "Is it possible that you are flying to Vietnam on this flight and coming straight back on the same plane?" – to which I said "Yes." His response was "I have never seen this done before. That's why the system is rejecting it." I got to Vietnam in the end and came straight back on the next flight. But this type of travel week on week takes its toll.

I remember on another occasion coming back on a flight one evening and getting chatting to the older lady in the seat beside me about my crazy travel arrangements. She turned and looked at me for a long time, and said, "You are going to kill yourself if you don't stop this." She explained that her son-in-law recently had suffered a massive heart attack on board a flight – he had the same lifestyle as me and she blamed it for his death. It made me think.

In my early years, I went from critically important event to critically important event, month after month, business after business, until I decided (read: my wife pointed out to me) there was no such thing as a critically important event in business. I just needed to figure out how to do things smarter and without always being the one to run to everyone else's beck and call as many successful business leaders do. There are always important events in business but I now make sure that I get the work / life balance right. It is more important to go to my children's nativity play at Christmas than to meet investors on the same day – so I move the meeting with the investors.

Don't get me wrong. I am not suggesting that, if you aim for global success, you will lose your family, but before you start the journey you need to make sure that you have the support of your family or partner in life and that you force some balance into your life.

Manage the risks

There is also the fear of losing what you have already achieved. Particularly in a recessionary market if you have had to bootstrap your business to get it to a point where you can now take a salary each month and the business is ticking along nicely, it is reasonable to ask whether you should risk all of this to accelerate the growth of your business.

At a meeting of CEOs who were accelerating the growth of their businesses, one of them said to me just that: "Do I risk everything I have achieved to date to grow my business?" It's a fair question.

Yes, there *are* plenty of risks associated with accelerating the growth of your business but, in my opinion, these risks can be managed, just like all the other risks that you have managed to date. The key is to be smart about how you accelerate the growth. Don't bet the farm on it, as they say. Often the perceived risks of growing are based on the current realities; by thinking through the risks as they appear today, you should be able to mitigate them and still grow your business if you are prepared to change the business model or share the profits, etc.

I met a CEO whose company was struggling to grow because of lack of capital. Most of his available funds were being used to fund hardware that was required for each new customer that the company deployed. By focusing on the problem, he was able to do a deal with a bank to offer three to five year finance agreements to the blue chip customers that he was selling to and his customers were happier owning the hardware. This fundamentally shifted his business up a gear by freeing up his cashflow and without giving up any profit.

So stop focusing on the risks to the point of doing nothing and start focusing on how to mitigate them with a view to accelerating the growth of your business.

You can do it if you believe you can

Your own perception of your own abilities as a CEO or business leader is critical. As Henry Ford said: "Whatever you think you can or you think you can't do, you are right."

Some years ago I met one of the most successful venture capitalists in Europe, whose success is legendary. In my first meeting with him, he asked me a simple question about the business I was pitching to him at the time: "Is this a billion dollar business?" My immediate and impulsive response was "Yes" and the conversation continued. After the meeting, I met another entrepreneur who had worked with the same VC who told me that the VC asked all new entrepreneurs the same question. Anyone who said "No" or hesitated before saying "Yes" was shown the door. His question was not really about the potential success of the business, but about the entrepreneur's state of mind. Unless you believe you can grow your business into a billion dollar business, you never will.

Learn to believe in yourself

One of the most common things that holds CEOs back from accelerating the growth of their business is fear: fear that you do not have the knowledge or skills to be a great CEO. At a meeting of some of the most successful CEOs that I have ever met, one privately admitted that he felt like a fake; he felt he did not possess real CEO skills and that he was just making it up as he went along – to which almost all of the other CEOs said that they felt exactly the same, but were afraid to admit it. There are no mysteriously brilliant CEOs out there who have all the right answers all of the time. We all make it up as we go along, but we get better at it over time as we learn what worked well and what did not work so well. So don't be held back by this unfounded fear; you would be surprised to know how many other CEOs that you admire share the same fear as you do (I did for many years).

Often the universe conspires to help you if you believe in your own success. A former chairman of one of my ventures, whom I respect, argues that great leaders who achieve great success for their business do not always have a perfect answer for what they need to do next, but they are prepared to step into the void, believing that a bridge will appear before them and that they will not fall down. They cannot see the bridge until they have taken that step and, if it does not appear, they know that they will fall to their death – but they believe that what they are doing will work out and, in the vast majority of cases, it does.

I am reminded of a story about a well-known professional golfer whose reply to a journalist's comment that "you seem to have had a lot of luck in that game" was "the more I practice, the luckier I get."

My leaps of faith seem to be less and less a leap and more a step as I get older and wiser. I can mitigate the risks and better predict the outcomes with less reliance on gut instinct and fate or leaving myself open to the mercy of the universe.

Making a difference

Apart from loving what you do as a business leader some entrepreneurs are motivated to simply make a difference. I want to make a difference: I want my companies to change the markets they operate in and to change customers' behaviors to help them improve how they do things by using our products or services. This concept is easier to understand in social entrepreneurship where, by definition, entrepreneurs are motivated to give something back to the society that we live in. But I have a friend who has been very successful in business: he has created, grown and exited a number of companies but is still motivated to create new companies and do it all over again. He told me that any company that he creates today must make a big difference to the world we live in or else he won't get involved – and these are for-profit companies, not charities.

Be passionate about what you do

I know it sounds like a cliché and can be overdone but I really believe that, if you are lucky enough to do something in business that you are passionate about, it can make a huge difference to your motivation and the ultimate results you achieve. People who are passionate about what they do make their work look easy and fun, simply because they love what they do. In venture capital pitches for raising money, I often heard VCs say that they are looking for people who are passionate about what they do in their company, because these people are more driven and focused on the results and so will achieve greater success.

I am fortunate to be passionate about what I do today. I love working on my current company, Digital Trading. I think our products are great, I know we have great people in the company and I can see that we are having a significant impact on our customers' ability to communicate and engage with their own customers. I can't describe Digital Trading as work or as a job, because I really enjoy every moment of what I do. I can go into my office at night and work till the late hours without thinking about it – it's not work, it's fun!

So if you can choose what your company does, try to pick something that you are passionate about – it can give you a significant competitive advantage.

3
LEADERSHIP

- Are great leaders born or are they created?
- Be a leader, not a manager
- Good leaders need to be authentic
- It's hard to be humble
- Give people a chance to do something they love
- What makes a good leader?
- What makes a bad leader?

Leadership is important because ...

If you can be a great leader of people you can achieve great things in life. No one person can create a hugely successful company on their own: you need others to work with you to deliver the great results that you are searching for. Being a great leader of people can have a significant impact on the potential results and achievements of your business because people go the extra mile for a great leader.

There are many examples of great leaders in our time: people like Nelson Mandela, who thousands of people were prepared to follow to make South Africa a great nation. Or Bob Geldof, who led millions of people to participate in the Live Aid concert and so collect millions of dollars for charity.

You don't need to be as great as either of them, but being able to lead a team of good people can have a huge impact on your ability to accelerate the growth of your company. It is important to be as good a leader as you can be, if you want to achieve great things in your company.

Are great leaders born or are they created?

Are great leaders born or do they become great leaders through learning and attaining positions of authority?

In my opinion great leaders are born but I believe good leadership also can be learned. Observe children: some are natural-born leaders, who can lead other children anywhere, because they always have something fun to do; they tell great stories; they listen to the other children's stories; and they look after them when they follow him/her. Watching the dynamics of children can teach us a lot about leadership, if you read what I wrote above as:

- "They tell great stories" equals "They have a great vision;"
- "They always have something fun to do" equals "This company is exciting to work for;"
- "They listen to the other children" equals "I matter in this business and my views are important;"
- "They looks after the other children" equals "The leader has our backs, I would follow him/her anywhere."

You may not be a natural-born leader but you can learn to do all of these things in your own business and become a very effective leader.

3: Leadership

Be a leader, not a manager

Many years ago, leadership came from positions of authority, which came from education, family inheritance, or wealth. I often think of the song *Fiddler on the Roof*, where Tevye says, "If you're rich, they think you really know." But today this type of leadership is less common, particularly now that everyone is educated and has a reasonable standard of living, equal rights, etc.

There is a significant difference between being a good and effective manager and being a good leader. Management is more about making decisions about how to use the resources in a business and how to plan the execution of tactics or strategies to achieve the objectives of the business. Leadership is more about inspiring people to follow and to believe in something greater than the task at hand.

I worked with two CEOs of factory-type businesses, helping them to create a new vision for their organizations. One shared his vision with his minimum wage workers; the other did not, for fear of them looking for a pay rise. I visited both factories and you could feel the culture that had been created by the CEO who chose to share his vision: his people worked with pride, greeted you as an equal and were happy to be part of something great where their work was important to the overall success of the business. The other factory was just a factory, which we inspected without engaging with any of the staff, who were all heads down when the CEO arrived. The difference between the two companies was down to the leadership.

Great leaders usually have a great vision and can align people to their vision and make them follow, not because they are in a position of authority but because people believe in them and what they stand for. A former chairman of one of my ventures used to say: "If you can inspire people to believe in your vision, then the world will conspire to help you." In other words, you can rally resources from anywhere, if the cause is big enough and if you can be an inspirational leader. I have used this to great effect in my own ventures. I have always been able to inspire people to believe in the vision of the business. When they do, they will perform way above what they believe to be their own ability.

Napoleon once said that "a leader is a dealer in hope." Getting people to believe in hope is a lethal weapon in business; it is the difference between organizations that just do the job and organizations that are passionate about succeeding and beating all the odds.

Some years ago, my company was involved in a long and contentious battle with one of the incumbent mobile operators in Ireland, where this company seemed to us to be doing everything it could to put us out of business because we were doing a better job than them as a mobile virtual network operator

(MVNO – a mobile telecoms operator that 'piggybacks' on another operator's network) on their own network. Every month, they would throw us another curveball to mess up our operations but the more they threw at us, the more resilient and the more resolved the entire company of over 150 people became. I saw some great people do some great things in that company because they believed in the vision and the cause. Our vision was simple: to provide the best cell phone service in Ireland (even though we did not own our own network or have the huge resources of our competitors).

Good leaders need to be authentic

To be a good leader, you need to be authentic; you need compassion for your followers; you need to lead from the front and to take the hits for your people and with your people. Great leaders are rarely motivated by their own self-interests; they look out for their people and generally make sure that they share both the pain and the gain.

Being an authentic leader is critically important to being a great leader. To be authentic you need to be real. I witnessed this going very wrong initially when I worked in a larger organization as a consultant, helping them with their strategy, after a new CEO was appointed from the existing management team. In his zest to show that he was a great leader, the new CEO decided to follow in the footsteps of a great and inspirational leader who is well known in the business world. But the mistake he made was to try to copy the great leader in every respect. Unfortunately, he fell flat on his face because everyone could see through this: they all knew him and what he was really like. The guy turned out to be a great CEO: once he dropped the pretense of being someone he was not, he became a very effective and good leader as a CEO and he commanded the respect of the staff for his honesty and integrity in listening and caring for his people – in other words, he became an authentic leader.

I remember a Jesuit teacher in my school telling me, "When everyone is someone, then no one is anyone." To stand out from the crowd and be a good leader requires something different today. For me, this is the ability to be authentic and to have some humility while inspiring people to follow a good cause or vision – otherwise we are all the same. If you want to learn more about leadership, I would recommend reading about Sir Ernest Shackleton, the great polar explorer, who saved his team from certain death through great leadership.

It's hard to be humble

One thing that you will see in all great leaders is humility. However, often this is a difficult ingredient to learn since humility is the ability to act as the lesser person when in fact you are the greater. Kipling's phrase, "If you can walk among kings and never lose the common touch," has stood to me over and over again. I have found that the most interesting people you meet in life are not the corporate high flyers, but the people on the ground: the cleaner, the taxi driver or the rookie software engineer. Often, they have great stories and are warm and welcoming.

One of my favorite forms of research, when I was dealing with mobile operators in different countries, was every time I visited a new country to meet a senior executive, I would talk to the taxi driver on the journey from the airport to the hotel or meeting. By the time I got there, I would know a lot about the market for cell phones, who was better, cheaper, etc. Many times, I would meet with the executive and tell him things that he did not know about his own business simply because he had lost touch with his customers, because he never spoke to them in a meaningful way.

When I worked in a mobile operator myself, I sent all of the senior managers out to the stores to meet real people. They were very uncomfortable with this, but it opened their eyes to what was happening on the ground and they had no choice but to listen to customers who came into the stores. The first thing I did myself when I joined the company was sit in the call center and listen for hours to the customer feedback. Again, this gave me huge insight into what needed to be done to fix some of the problems that the company was having at the time.

You would be surprised at how many times I was inspired or a new idea was triggered from a conversation with a low-ranking employee who just cut to a problem that they were seeing on the ground and that the senior managers could not or would not see.

Give people a chance to do something they love

One thing that has worked for me as a leader is giving people a chance to do something that they always wanted to do. I have taken people from one role and put them into a new role that they wanted to do and that they were passionate about but maybe had no experience or specific skills in. In every case they said, "I don't think I can do this" but without exception, they all excelled and did a much better job that anyone who was in the same role with all the experience and skills. There is no more powerful formula to achieve supernormal performance than finding passion and combining it with a personal challenge to succeed.

Good leaders challenge people to do more than they believe they are capable of doing themselves. When they achieve what they believed was an impossible goal, just watch them grow and perform for you and the business.

What makes a good leader?

In my opinion good and effective leaders possess some or all of these traits:

- **Compassion:** They know how to listen to their people with compassion and understanding;
- **Confidence:** They are confident about their vision and how the business will grow – even where they are not totally certain about how things will work out, they never show this;
- **Friendliness:** Having time for everyone; making them feel important by addressing them by their first name; looking people in the eye and focusing on them alone;
- **Respect:** Having time and respect for other people's opinions, culture, health, family, etc. All these issues are part of our everyday lives that make us who and what we are in work. I don't think you can ignore the whole person when they come to work, but if you embrace the whole person through respecting their wider being you can achieve much higher performance and commitment from them;
- **Appreciation:** Everyone needs to be appreciated; it costs nothing to say "Thanks" and to show appreciation to your team. Yes, it costs time, which is scarce in any busy organization, but the power of appreciation is completely underused by leaders in business. By saying "Job well done" or "Thanks" sincerely, you can motivate people to do more, to enjoy their work, to feel valued and respected, all of which can be channeled into higher performance and commitment to your vision or goals.

What makes a bad leader?

I have worked with some very bad leaders, people who got themselves into positions of authority simply because they were very good at their job. Bad leadership can kill a company in a matter of months. When a bad leader is appointed to an organization, within a very short time the whole culture changes, people fight with each other; they are not motivated to go the extra mile so they 'work to rule' and begin to see their work as a task they must complete as opposed to mastering their skills.

Many years ago, I worked for an absolute tyrant, who screamed at everyone – including me. She was brilliant at her job but, in just one year, she lost a team of over 15 people by screaming at and disrespecting every one of them. Eventually I also left (telling the managing director what I thought as I did so) but it took the business another year of this behavior to eventually realize that this bad leader was the problem and to fire her.

Being good at a job does not make you a good leader; and bad leaders can do tremendous damage by demotivating an entire team or business. No matter how brilliant they are at their job, they cannot carry the entire business on their own shoulders.

I think it is important to know what makes a bad leader:

- **Bullying:** Bad leaders are often bullies in work, undermining people they work with and using bullying tactics to make them complete tasks;
- **Lack of trust:** Bad leaders set people up to compete with each other as opposed to working together; people stop trusting one another because the so-called leader has created a culture of fear of being found out if something goes wrong;
- **All stick and no carrot:** Bad leaders use fear as their main form of motivation: "If you don't do this well, I will fire you;" they never try to motivate people through positive feedback; even when they pay bonuses, there's always a catch;
- **Lack of integrity and compassion:** Bad leaders don't care about the people they work with; to them, people are resources like machines: do a task and you get fed, don't and you get fired.

Don't be a bad leader. Don't have one on your team.

4
VISION

- How to entice people away from the giants
- Keep it short and simple
- Your vision can inspire stakeholders
- Wrong vision? Change it
- Small steps, not big leaps
- Being true to your vision is not easy
- If you achieve your vision, what's next?

Vision is important because ...

Great leaders inspire people with their vision. So having a vision for your business is a critical component for achieving accelerated growth-type success – but note that a vision is not your mission statement and it is not your strategy.

Your vision is all about where you see your business in a number of years from now: how big can it be, what markets can you dominate; what products will people know you for and what will you have achieved. Your vision is the most powerful weapon that you have in your armory to motivate your people, your customers, your partners, your investors, your suppliers and your family.

In my view, it is very difficult to accelerate the growth of your company without a clear and simple vision that people believe in (because it is exciting or important and also possible to achieve).

How to entice people away from the giants

In a small company that is taking on giants, you need to attract good people who are not afraid to fight the giants. They probably work for a giant today, so how do you get them to leave the safe haven of the giant's den and to follow you into a much less safe place, with probably lower benefits or salary and probably to work harder and longer hours in some relatively dingy office compared to their previous luxury? It's your vision that will inspire them to join you. You would be amazed at how many people can be inspired to take risks if they believe that the journey will be full of fun and excitement and they could make some money along the way.

I once met a very well known CEO of a very large company who told me that he had been approached by Richard Branson at a time when the CEO was working in a very safe and reasonably well-paid job in a big corporation. Branson asked him to join him in a new venture and for all the right reasons he said "No." But Branson did not take "No" for an answer: he invited the CEO and his wife to his home and, after a fun-packed weekend and a glimpse of the new world that was possible through the eyes of a great entrepreneur and a great vision, he accepted the job. I think the CEO's wife had a lot to do with his decision, as I am sure Richard Branson knew full well – but to this day, this person has never looked back.

People love to be part of a greater cause, a vision that was made possible by the sheer determination, passion and hard work of a team of people who believed in what they could do and what they could change, often despite the odds. These are the types of companies that change the world. Google, Facebook, YouTube and all the names that we know today did things so differently at the time they entered the market with a bunch of guys who

4: Vision

believed that there was a better way through their own vision of what the world could look like if they succeeded. It is hard to believe what these companies have achieved in such little time. They are now the giants – but you are the next generation of challengers to what is now their established model.

Keep it short and simple

Your vision does not need to be complex or long-winded. In fact, the simpler, the better. For example, say: "We want to be the number one X in the world."

I used the words "want to be." I could have used the words "will be" instead. My mother always said to me when I was young that "you are what you say you are." I have used this many times in my life and to great effect. Believe me, anyone can do this – by saying you are the person you are, you tend to get closer to where you want to be; when you are there, you figure out very quickly how to do things.

So set the vision for your own business: be bold but also be realistic, and you will be amazed at what you can achieve. For example, Henry Ford had a clear and simple vision: "To make a car that every household in America can afford." Although this vision was a stretch of the imagination at the time he set it, he proved it was possible – and achieved it.

Your vision can inspire stakeholders

A good vision is important to inspire all of your stakeholders that you need to grow your business, like key suppliers. I am very fond of 'chicken and egg, which comes first?' businesses – where you need lots of customers before you get lots of suppliers, but you need lots of suppliers before you get lots of customers. Almost all of my businesses were like this. In this situation, you need to be able to show people on both sides of the equation your vision of what the world will look like when you get to where you want to be.

One of my businesses was involved in selling a digital media service to mobile operators all over the world (retailing games, music, apps, etc.), but before the mobile operators would buy from us they wanted to see that we had all the major content owners signed up, while the content owners would only deal with us if we could prove that we had all the mobile operators already signed up. So we had to create the situation where each side believed that the other was on board through how we articulated our vision. By the time they got to contract stage we had managed the two sides of the equations in perfect harmony and solved the riddle of the chicken and egg – they both arrived at the very same time.

Wrong vision? Change it

Often, your vision can be wrong. If it is, change it. Unlike your strategy which is expected to change, your vision is much more difficult to change and there are consequences such as your people losing faith, your suppliers getting very confused or even walking away, but if you call the market wrong or your vision is not achievable in the time frame relevant to the business then call it and change.

In one of my businesses, I had a vision that everyone would listen to their newspaper in their cars or on the train using an MP3 player, having downloaded the paper to their PC overnight. That was more than 10 years ago. Now, we have the iPhone and the AppStore with 'all you can eat' video and audio content. At the time, no one was buying; everyone said it was a great idea and maybe some day they would buy it. But I needed them to buy then so I could pay salaries and get a return on my latest investment (for which, by the way, I had remortgaged my home). After two years, I had to admit failure and change tack to become a content aggregator like many others at the time. We made the transition and lived to tell the tale, with the company ultimately being sold successfully. We simply were ahead of our time.

Small steps, not big leaps

Consumers rarely take leaps of faith and jump into something completely new; they prefer to take gentle steps. Be prepared for this and, if needs be, take gentle steps yourself. Create a strategy that brings customers on a series of small step changes from where they are today along the way to get to where your vision might be. This will allow you to create a profitable business on the way.

I had my own experience of this when we were selling a digital media service to mobile operators through a company called iO. Our solution was all-singing and all-dancing, with music, videos and much more. We sold it into one of the major African markets, while a smaller company offered the same operator a much more basic SMS-based content service that we could have supplied but did not as I thought it was too basic and far removed from my vision. In the first year of trading, the other company did several million dollars worth of business with this operator but we did very little. In hindsight, we should have covered the basic service as well as the advanced visionary services; it would have been much more profitable and ultimately more successful for achieving the vision of our business.

I worked with a CEO of a company who had a vision to be the world leader in supplying stock video clips. He had this vision many years earlier, but he was too early and the market was not ready for video. He did not change his vision, but he had to change his strategy and became a supplier of stock photos to generate cash to build the business. Today, he is the market leader for stock video, in a still fast-growing market, but he still sells a lot of photos to fund his vision of a time when video sales will exceed photo sales in the market.

Being true to your vision is not easy

Having a great vision that inspires people to follow you and achieve it can be a very difficult path. If your vision is truly 'visionary,' then many people will laugh at you or challenge your ability to achieve it.

This can be very difficult: for example, if you need to raise money from venture capitalists who cannot see your vision becoming a reality, then they won't fund you. I have had this problem with most of my companies: my vision was not shared by the investors in the early stages so I could not raise funds from traditional sources. Later, as the vision became a reality, lots of investors wanted to invest in the business but by then we did not need their money.

The same is happening to me today. Thank God I don't need to raise investment to grow my company Digital Trading, though early on I did speak to a number of investors who simply could not see my vision becoming a reality – Customer Relationship Engagement (CRE) becoming a huge market with every enterprise using this or a similar service.

So don't expect everyone to share your vision, particularly in the early years as you work to make it a reality, but be prepared to do whatever is necessary to fund and achieve your vision. I often think of the guys in Shazam, the music discovery application that finds tunes that you are listening to. I met them years ago when they were trying to sell their vision and very few people believed it was possible to achieve; they are now the market leader and their business is huge because their vision became a reality.

If you achieve your vision, what's next?

When you have achieved your vision I hope you are sitting at the helm of a very large company that has accelerated its growth and achieved great things in the process. But if you have achieved a great vision and have not replaced it with a new vision, your business can start to slow down or even fail.

I mentioned earlier Henry Ford's vision to build a car that every household in America could afford. He achieved this vision by focusing on making the cheapest car in the market with no frills – not even a choice of color; it came only in black. But as other competitors like Chrysler entered the market, offering cars with luxuries and color options, consumers quickly moved to these cars, leaving

Ford with a dwindling market share – the company almost collapsed at one point. Ford needed a new vision to inspire workers and stakeholders to strive for something great again.

Once you achieve your vision for your company, you need to create a new one – as before, one that inspires all the stakeholders to achieve the next level of greatness and also is realistic and achievable.

5
STRATEGY

- Strategy is ever-changing
- Your competitors will copy you – accept it
- If it is not working, change it
- Strategy is neither your vision nor your mission statement
- Different strategies for success

Strategy Important because ...

Strategy is very important to your business success and to accelerating its growth.

When I went to college to study business, I was intrigued and excited about the prospects of learning how to 'do business strategy'. I had an expectation that it was going to be like learning how to build your own crystal ball, which could see into the future and help you to predict how things could be shaped by an organization to take advantage of the forecasted changes. I searched hard for this mysterious tool called strategy; I looked at and learned many different theories, from many learned professors and authors, but as hard as I tried I still could not get a handle on this elusive thing called strategy.

It was not until I went into business on my own that I began to learn what strategy really was. It is not a magical crystal ball or a process that can be learned from textbooks; it is the ability to decide on tactics and decisions that give you a competitive advantage.

For example, innocent smoothies decided to go for mass-market brand-building, achieved through traditional media advertising – an expensive decision, but it worked. Look at how innocent has differentiated itself from the thousands of other companies that make smoothies. Starbucks decided to make its stores the 'third place' in your life – the first being home, the second being work and the third being Starbucks – so it introduced couches, easy listening music, free Wi-Fi, etc and it worked. Again, look at how Starbucks has differentiated itself from the thousands of coffee shops all over the world.

Strategy is ever-changing

Your strategy generally needs to keep changing – typically, it has a 'sell by' date. It is designed to get you to a certain point; once you reach it, then you will need to change your strategy to get to the next point or milestone.

In the early days of your business, your strategy might be to prove the benefits of your service to a first customer; then the next phase of your strategy would be to use this customer as a reference to win the next customer who will make you a profit; then your strategy becomes perfecting your business model to accelerate the growth of your business by replicating sales through scalable channels.

I did this in iO. We won a tiny customer as a reference customer. We practically gave the customer the service for free and put lots of resources into creating a success for them, but we never had an expectation of making money from them. We always intended using them as a reference customer to help us to win the next customer, a slightly larger customer, who made us money. We then appointed BT as a sales channel to scale this up once we had proven the model with the early customers and we went on to win larger customers. This effectively was our go-to-market (sales) strategy (see **Chapter 11**).

Your competitors will copy you – accept it

If you have a strategy that gives you a competitive advantage and you achieve higher levels of success, your competitors will copy you. Imitation is the highest form of flattery, as they say. I have been copied by my competitors over and over again. In my early days, I was absolutely incensed by this and wanted to go out and find the person who copied me and to tell them to go get their own strategy and stop copying me (in less polite language). But over the years, I have learned that this is what you should expect if you get your strategy right. If you get it wrong, no one will copy you – so, to a large degree, copying is a barometer of how successful your strategies are. Don't get stressed out by it: recognize that, if the competition copies you, your strategy must be working and hurting them by taking business from them. Worry more if they don't copy you, since it means they don't think much of your strategy.

When I worked for Meteor, a mobile operator that had been locked out of the market by litigation while the market matured from 45% to over 95% penetration, the task of winning consumers seemed almost impossible given that the company had less coverage, smaller marketing budget, fewer retail outlets, etc. But a simple and carefully planned strategy made this company a huge success and brought it from nothing to winning over 20% of the Irish market.

By standing back from the problem and thinking carefully about the market that we could win, with the service that we could deliver, at a price that made sense, we were able to create the most compelling proposition for younger pre-paid customers that the market had ever seen. We offered 'all you could eat' SMS for 30 days to anyone who topped up by €20 each month – the catch was that both sender and receiver had to be on the Meteor network. This strategy was designed to bring urban-based youth to the network by creating a herd instinct where groups, who communicated with each other a lot using SMS, all moved together to benefit from the free texts. Today, all the other operators have copied this model because it was so successful at winning new subscribers – and now that they have, it is again very difficult to differentiate which network's offer is the best.

As your competitors copy a successful strategy, you need to take the next step to stay ahead or eventually you will be left behind by someone with a better strategy. So your strategy will be ever-changing if you are in a competitive market and your strategies are working to your advantage.

If it is not working, change it

In a growing business you must be prepared to chop and change your strategy. If what you are doing is not working, or if the competition reacts and takes the advantage, you must change your strategy.

Being small is a huge competitive advantage that many companies wanting to scale underestimate. Larger companies are envious of how agile and fast-responding smaller companies can be to market changes or customer demand. As a smaller company you should excel at reading market changes and moving fast to take a competitive advantage or to deliver a service that the market wants faster than your slow-moving larger competitors.

When I joined Meteor it was charging the same prices for international calls as all the other mobile networks – something in the region of €2.50 per minute to call Australia. When I looked at the costs for this call, I found we were paying no more than 5 cents to place the call to Australia so I decided to change our pricing strategy to get people from other countries living in Ireland to move to Meteor and make their calls home using our mobile network instead of a payphone or a fixed line. So we dropped the price to around 25 cents per minute, the same price as calling other cell phones within Ireland. This was an easy decision for us: we started with very little international traffic and, even at these very low rates, we were still making huge margins. Our competitors couldn't copy us as a price drop of this size would destroy their enormous profits from international calls. It took a while before our revenues started to grow, as communities of foreign nationals in Ireland started to switch to our network to avail of these compelling international rates. Years later, when it was too late, the competition copied us.

Strategy is not your vision nor your mission statement

Your strategy is neither your vision nor your mission statement. We commonly hear these terms used interchangeably, as if they were all the same.

We looked earlier at your vision. And a mission statement often is no more than a chunk of text that large corporations frame and hang all on their office walls to impress their own employees and the occasional customer. Mostly the employees are not inspired by this, yet management can feel good that they have a mission statement and the consultants can sell more ideas to the company.

OK, this might be a little harsh but if you are accelerating the growth of your business, you don't need a mission statement, while you do need a vision and a strategy. Get your priorities right.

Different strategies for success

Strategy cuts across everything you do in your business: from your products and services strategy, your sales and marketing strategy, your go-to-market strategy, your partnership strategy, your finance strategy, etc. In fact, every aspect of the business can be strategic to the growth of the business if you want it to be. Here are some examples:

- **Finance:** Many companies do not treat finance as a strategic component of the business but it can be. For example, many US companies raise lots of cash and then buy other companies in the same market, accelerating their growth through sheer dominance. They use finance as a strategic weapon, hiring the best people as CFOs, always raising more and more cash with a view to getting a listing (IPO) to further fuel their accelerated growth. Are you using finance as a strategic tool in your business? Could you buy your way to success if you could raise enough money? If you raise lots of money, can you hold onto some equity and make sure you get a good return?

- **Operations:** I use my operations strategy as a key competitive advantage to maximize the profitability of Digital Trading because I am funding it myself. Using cloud hosting, remote working, online communications, SaaS services from key suppliers, etc, we can create a dynamic and scalable company that can work with and service customers anywhere in the world at a fraction of the cost of any of our competitors. As we grow the business, this operations strategy will create a very profitable company over time;

- **Corporate Social Responsibility (CSR):** In a world where consumers hold companies accountable for their actions, companies that are seen to take responsibility for the community and the world they work in can get a hugely positive increase in productivity, PR, sales, etc by adopting good CSR practices. CSR is about giving back: some companies offer free services or give their staff time to work for charities, etc; in Digital Trading, we give a significant part of our resources to support MyGoodPoints. It is part of who we are as a company and, even though it is not designed to directly impact our profitability (in fact, it costs us money all the time), in the longer term because our people are very motivated and passionate about who we are and what we do, it makes for a more successful company;

- **Marketing:** I look at marketing in more detail in **Chapter 10**, because it can offer a hugely strategic weapon in beating your competition if you use it well. Why does Coca Cola constantly beat the competition for soft drinks? There are many products out there that arguably taste as good as Coke, but it is Coca Cola's marketing strategy that keeps it in pole position – the company is brilliant at marketing. Yes, it requires deep pockets to create this level of brand awareness, but you could adopt the same strategy, albeit starting on a smaller scale, using marketing to drive your products or services through to customers and to beat the competition.

SECTION 2
THE COMPONENTS OF ACCELERATED GROWTH

6

SUMMARIZING WHAT YOU DO IN AN ELEVATOR PITCH

- Standardize your pitch
- Focus on measurable impact
- Cut out excess words
- Differentiate yourself from competitors
- Credibility is key
- Don't pitch when you're not ready
- Even when you have time for a full pitch, start with your elevator pitch
- Make your pitch compelling
- How to stand out with your elevator pitch

Your elevator pitch is important because ...

A whole chapter to something as small and basic as an elevator pitch – why? Because it is so important to your ability to accelerate the growth of your business.

An elevator pitch is what you would say to pitch your business to someone in the time it takes an elevator to go from the first floor to the top floor of a building. You need to be able to describe your business in one or two sentences so that anyone listening, including your grandmother, can understand what you do.

Time and time again, I meet CEOs and business leaders who simply cannot tell me in a few sentences what their business does. I am sure you have experienced this yourself: you meet someone and ask them what they do and they give you a 'blah' answer. It's a missed opportunity to do business together.

Everyone you meet, as you continue to grow your business, needs to receive your elevator pitch in some shape or form, whether they are potential investors, potential customers or potential exit partners. Getting this right can make a significant difference to the success of your business.

My own business today started out selling an innovative service that allows an enterprise to communicate with its customers using SMS, email, voice, etc. We initially called it an "Applied Unified Communications" service, since it allowed an enterprise to apply unified communications to solving business problems. Needless to say, everyone scratched their heads at this; they didn't understand what we meant. As customers purchased the service (slowly), they compared it to CRM, so we started calling it CRM and selling a CRM story. But the CRM market is very crowded and typically CRM solutions are very complex, so we could never be credible as a new entrant trying to make a name for ourselves in it. Instead, we focused on making it "Simple CRM" and coined the phrase "Customer Relationship Engagement" or CRE to differentiate us from the CRM market. We now describe this as "next generation simple-to-use CRM, where enterprises and their customers can engage in two-way communications that are targeted, personalized and permission-based." Everyone understands it, because it is close to the current CRM market, but yet we describe a unique value proposition that is compelling. So far so good: we are accelerating our growth and lots of customers are signing up for the service, including global brands that sell and use complex CRM services – so we must be doing something right.

Standardize your pitch

If you have ever attended a trade show where one after another people come up to you and ask you what you do, think about the variety of answers that you give, or worse still, think about the variety of answers that all the people who work for you may give. Walk around your office and ask people from different parts of the business "What do we do?" You will be amazed at the variety of answers you get, including probably a few "I have no clue what we do."

If you are serious about accelerating the growth of your business, everyone in the company, including finance and engineering, must know what you do and all of them must be able to tell someone they meet why the company is so great to work for or with.

It's particularly critical that salespeople get this right, since they are the people who meet customers. How can a sales person articulate the business' elevator pitch if they have not been told what it is? Don't let them make it up as they go along. Your quality of service, customer support, marketing support, innovation etc., all of which form the full value proposition for your customer and the differentiators from your competitors, need to be clearly articulated by your sales team if the potential customer is to buy from you.

Focus on measurable impact

To be compelling, your elevator pitch needs to articulate a significant and measurable impact on the customer's business – for example, "if you buy our product, you could reduce your cost of operations by 30%," or "if you sold our products, you could reduce your current customer loss rate by 20%," or "our products represent 30% of your competitors' revenues and they make a gross margin of 50%, how would this impact your revenues and margins?" If it is not compelling, they will walk away and you may never hear from them again.

In my own CRE pitch, I tell enterprise customers that the days of CRM (where typically a company 'manages' the relationship that they want to have with a customer) are gone: you now need to engage with customers in two-way communications that are targeted and personalized; you cannot tell customers what you want them to hear any more; and you must treat them as equals. This is compelling and gets their attention because they know it is true in this new connected digital media world.

Cut out excess words

When you are creating your elevator pitch, avoid generic terms like 'platform' or 'product.' Focus on the benefits. Try to cut back the number of words after you have written the first version of the elevator pitch so you get your message across in the fewest words you can – it might be a short elevator ride!

On a sales training program delivered by one of the major FMCG companies, their sales people were taught how to create an elevator pitch for their products. They used an example of a fish store, where the exercise was to create the wording for the sign on the storefront. The sign started out as "Fresh Fish Sold Daily", the objective being to tell customers that the store sold fish and that it was always fresh. The trainer argued that "sold" was unnecessary, as the fact that it was a store meant that it sold things. So the sign became "Fresh Fish Daily". Again, the trainer argued that no one would sell fish that was not fresh. In the end, the wording on the sign was narrowed to just "Fish" on the basis that everything else was implied and accepted by the customer.

Differentiate yourself from competitors

You also need to consider what is different between what you offer and what your competitors offer. Assume your target customer is already using your main competitor's product/service. What would you say to get their CEO's attention? What would be compelling about your product/service over and above your competitor's?

You gain a significant advantage if you know the stated goals of the CEO and your company can help them attain these goals. Publicly-quoted companies state their goals and growth ambitions in their annual reports. Read them and tweak your elevator pitch to different companies based on their stated growth strategies.

Credibility is key

It is often important to establish credibility in your elevator pitch, particularly if you are a smaller or unheard-of company. You can achieve this by referencing significant customers or case studies that the listener may know, or use your own case study – for example, "our solution delivered an ROI of 500% for XYZ who are a much smaller company than you, do the math."

But a word of warning, if you get access to a key decision-maker and you have something compelling to offer, get the credibility part nailed before you pitch; otherwise, you could blow your chances of ever getting back to the table.

Another way to deal with this is to give the pitch but hold off selling to the target. Just mark their cards – for example, "We are going to do x over the coming 12 months, watch this space." When you do the x and it is meaningful to the target, then you can go back and say "Remember me, I told you I was going to do x. I did x and now I'd like to talk to you about applying this to your business."

Don't pitch when you're not ready

Although I err on the side of meeting everyone and turning over every rock, prepared or not, because you never know what you might find underneath it, if I know I am not ready for the big pitch I often just work on the relationship, or focus on something interesting as a conversation that they will remember as significant, making a personal impression, which opens the door to the elevator pitch at a later stage.

It can be hard to resist the temptation of pitching to your dream customer particularly if they are standing beside you or you have just been introduced to them. I have learned the hard way that, if I am not ready for the pitch, then I should hold off until I am.

In Digital Trading, I believe that in time we could develop a very significant strategic partnership with one of the idnustry's largest players. Although I have met many of their senior executives and was offered the opportunity to meet the key decision-maker in our segment, I declined the offer knowing that we have not developed the business far enough to be ready for a strategic partnership. So we wait. When I believe we are ready, then I will make the approach backed with a compelling value proposition that has been proven and measured with key performance indicators (KPIs) that prove how successful our business will be if we can scale through a partnership.

Even when you have time for the full pitch, start with your elevator pitch

Even when you know you have time to explain your business properly, start with an elevator pitch that captures as much as possible about the business in an overview. Then help your audience to understand exactly what you do by using a video, photos, screenshots, demos, etc before you get into the detail of your presentation or discussion.

I have been in many meetings where initially we were allocated a lot of time to give a full pitch for our business but, at the last minute, we were told that the time had been shortened to 10 or 20 minutes. Or we started our pitch and the audience decided to take us in a different direction with questions that didn't allow us to get back on track to our pitch.

To avoid getting caught out like this and potentially never getting the opportunity to tell your full story, start by using the elevator pitch to get the full story out on the table before you go on a journey that could take you anywhere. This also helps to keep the audience focused on the key areas, because they know where you are going with the full pitch and won't get lost along the way.

Make your pitch compelling

Assuming you put in all the work to perfect your elevator pitch as outlined above, don't fall at the final hurdle: make sure you deliver it well and make it compelling to the listener. If you are not excited about your business and the scale of the opportunity, then how do you expect your audience to get excited about it? Your excitement needs to show in your delivery. Speaking in low tones, with no animation, using no pictures or tangible examples, can turn a great and well-researched pitch into something that your audience will switch off from.

US CEOs are known for delivering great presentations. When I worked with the UK Trade & Investment team, the one thing they repeatedly highlighted was the inability of UK companies to present themselves and their companies in a great light. In many cases, the UK businesses could build better products than the Americans but they failed to communicate this to the world, so US companies continued to win in the market.

The same is true of Irish companies. On a recent visit of Silicon Valley investors to Ireland, they remarked: "When you see a pitch from an American CEO, they sell you the Ferrari, but when you open the hood you find a Ford engine. But the Irish CEO sells you a Ford, you open the hood and find a Ferrari engine."

You need to get your pitch right and sell it like you are selling a Ferrari, regardless of what is under the hood. Both the packaging and perceptions matter. Don't take a chance on getting this wrong. If you need to practice your pitch in front of the mirror or with your life partner or with total strangers, do it.

How to stand out with your elevator pitch

It is worth noting that we live in a world of pitches. If you are a buyer of products or services in a business, you constantly see pitches from suppliers; if you are an investor, you constantly see pitches.

So, if you are the person pitching, how do you make your pitch stand out from the crowd? Some companies are now adopting a more visual and tactile approach to pitches, adding something memorable (even surprising) to get the audience's attention. So, for example, if you make a product that people can consume, then let them taste it; if you make a physical product, let them see it and touch it; if you build software, let the audience demo it themselves. Or, for impact, do something memorable like setting off fireworks or show a funny video clip, as long as it is relevant to your pitch.

I have seen many examples of over-the-top pitches: some worked very well but they can backfire badly on you if they go wrong. Make sure you know your audience and that what you do is both relevant and memorable. In this way, standing out from the crowd will give you a higher chance of winning.

How to capture your elevator pitch in your Accelerated Growth Plan slide deck ...

The objective behind your elevator pitch is to give the recipient a complete overview of who you are and what you do, making it compelling for them to want to find out more or better still to engage with your company immediately.

Your elevator pitch is an extended version of your value proposition and should capture areas that the value proposition may not cover, while still remaining short and compelling.

Your pitch might start by establishing your credibility, saying that "we are the supplier of A to companies X, Y and Z," before moving to your value proposition. You might close on a compelling call-to-action: "And we can supply you with this service for significantly less than you currently pay to our competitors."

Use your elevator pitch in your opening slide for your accelerated growth plan. Make your text fit on one slide. Where possible, separate the 'what we do' from the 'how we do it.' So, for example, "our software allows your business to completely automate the insurance claim process."

Try to create an elevator pitch for your company keeping the whole pitch to one or two sentences that you could say in about two minutes. Test this out on people and see if they get it; if they don't, then continue to refine it; over time, it will get better until it becomes part of your company's natural language that everyone speaks.

7
COMMUNICATING YOUR VALUE PROPOSITION TO YOUR CUSTOMERS

- Do your own research – ask your customers
- Let the customer tell you where the value lies
- Uncommoditize your products
- Value propositions are not based on cost
- Consider your value chain
- Where is your focus in the value chain?
- Your value proposition must be compelling to your customers
- The importance of perceived value
- Understand your customer's constraints
- Measure and prove your benefits
- Competing with limited resources means listening to customers
- Keep it simple, stupid!

Your value proposition is important because ...

Many people believe that the value proposition is simply the product or service that you sell. No, the value proposition is the product/service *plus* the whole wrapping, whistles and bells.

I learned about value propositions on the street, where all good learning takes place. I was from the midlands in Ireland and I went to college in Cork. At the time, there was a huge oversupply of mushrooms in the midlands and a huge shortage in the south; as a result, the difference in price was enormous. So being an entrepreneur, I decided to start trading in mushrooms. Even with a significant margin for myself, I could offer the potential customer a fresher and better presented product, with potential for a 500% mark-up on my price. I put on an old suit that my uncle had given to me as a hand-me-down and I set out to sell this compelling value proposition to the retailers in Cork, mainly supermarkets and butchers. One by one I went in, asked for the owner and gave them my pitch, but everyone rejected my offer, saying, "Your mushrooms are great but I can't buy them from you because I buy my tomatoes, lettuce and other vegetables from the same supplier as my mushrooms. They give me the variety and the service that I need. Sorry." I tried lots of different retailers and I got the same reply from all of them. No matter how compelling my single product was, it was not enough to make them change suppliers because they got so many other benefits from their current supplier and they did not want to upset this relationship. Walking back to college, defeated in my pursuit of entrepreneurship, I passed a fruit and vegetable wholesaler. I decided to chance my arm and go in with my value proposition. To my amazement, the owner jumped at the deal and ordered 300 boxes of mushrooms as his first order for delivery the next day, as opposed to the 10 or so boxes I might have sold to a small retailer. By the end of the day, I had visited all of the fruit and vegetable wholesalers in Cork and had sold in excess of 500 boxes, giving up a small amount of my margin in the process but hugely up saleswise on where I had expected to be. It was a great business: every day, I was on the college payphone feeding in coins as I matched supply to demand and made an excellent profit in the process.

But it taught me two key lessons about value propositions:
- It is not all about the product or service, it is also about support, packaging, marketing, relationships, location, guarantees, etc;
- The value proposition worked for a different type of business where the product quantity, quality and price were what mattered to them.

So when you look at your own value proposition, what can you see today, what is the product or service you sell today, how do you package and market this service, how do you support your customers and what other value added services do you deliver?

Do your own research – ask your customers

On one of the CEO programs that I attended, all the CEOs were asked to contact at least five customers and to ask them why they bought from the CEO's company. It was interesting to hear the CEOs' views of their value proposition before they did the customer research and then afterwards.

I cannot overemphasize the importance of you, as the business leader or CEO, doing your own research. Don't go out and hire a market research agency. The best type of research any company executive can do is to sit and listen to their own customers; from this, you will hear their problems and you will hear the benefits that they see in your products and services. This is incredible insight into helping you to accelerate the growth of your business.

I spent most of my first week as a senior executive of a mobile operator (Meteor) sitting in the call center listening to and talking to existing customers. When I re-joined the directors in the boardroom, I knew what was good and bad about the business. By listening to our customers, we could identify clearly where we could excel and win good business, by focusing on the youth pre-paid market in urban areas and building communities of users on the network, which ultimately allowed us to accelerate the growth of the business.

Let the customer tell you where the value lies

A CEO who sold technology to companies to help them retail their products online told me that his technology was well priced and easy for them to install and set up for the customer. When he spoke to his customers, none of them referred to these benefits; they all referred to the fact that his technology was so easy to use that they could turn around a new retailing campaign in hours as opposed to weeks. This let them react much faster to competitors, a huge benefit to the customer and a huge competitive advantage for the CEO's company when he compared his product to the other suppliers of similar solutions. This feedback allowed the CEO to measure the benefit and offer it as a compelling value proposition to his customers to accelerate the growth of his company.

When I owned a company called Meridian Communications that supplied cell phone services to enterprise customers, the key difference that was valued most by the customers was the level of customer service that we offered compared to other suppliers of cell phones at the time. Simply helping customers to understand how to use the technology, what price plans to buy and what phones to use was a huge benefit to these enterprises. It proved to be a huge competitive advantage to our business, which did not have the huge networks or marketing budgets of the big boys. Simply listening to the customer and giving them what they want in a profitable way can drive a business towards growth.

Uncommoditize your products

You need to differentiate your products or services from all your competitors by making your value proposition strategically important to your target customers.

I met the CEO of a company that was offering renewable energy to large enterprises. Its business model was to build and operate a wind turbine on the site of a large enterprise that consumed lots of electricity. The value proposition was focused on offering better prices for the electricity for a guaranteed period of time to hedge the rising cost of oil and other energy. A good business model but difficult to sell because it was dependent on targeting significant users of electricity where the electricity cost was a large proportion of the overall cost of production; when the company found these potential customers, they were competing with all the other electricity suppliers in a liberalized market where they could compete only on price. This was a commodity product in a commodity market.

So the challenge was to make the product/service strategic to the business owner, instead of selling to the procurement guy who buys electricity. The CEO decided to focus on enterprise customers with consumer-facing products or services that used a lot of electricity in their production. Telling their consumers that their products or services were 'wind-made' helped these businesses to gain a competitive advantage in the market by implementing a corporate social responsibility (CSR) strategy that the consumer could relate to. The company quickly won a customer: a beer company that saw the value of telling its customers that its products used wind energy created on its own site to produce the beer. Today, the company is targeting more of these types of customers to help them to accelerate the growth of its business through an enhanced value proposition.

Value propositions are not based on cost

The value proposition to the customer has nothing to do with the cost of creating the product or service; often, the value associated with the wrapping or service trimmings is more important than the product or service itself. For example, in a cosmetic company, the value proposition includes the brand, associations with and endorsements by celebrities, the packaging, the advertising and the wrapping. In fact, it's more about what's outside the bottle than what's inside.

In my first company, I manufactured and sold a premium aftershave called Nautique. I used an outsourced manufacturer, which produced cosmetics for a number of well-known brands at the time, to make a unique product. Between the product and the packaging, the production cost of each bottle of aftershave was approximately IR£2 but it retailed for IR£36. The difference was marketing – to convince the buyer that paying nearly 20 times more for an aftershave than it cost to produce was still a compelling value proposition, one they should buy again and again.

The value proposition for a premium branded product is as much about the customer service, the packaging, the location of the service, its design, etc. as it is about the actual product itself. Look at how Apple has dominated the smartphone market and still commands a huge premium for its cell phones in a market where its competitors offer better technologies at much lower prices.

Consider your value chain

When you examine your value proposition, consider the value chain involved in delivering your products or services to the market. This important component needs to be clearly understood if you are to accelerate the growth of your business.

For example, when I was a child one of the greatest treats in my week was when my parents asked me to go to the bakery in our town and buy some sweet buns. I loved to look at the beautiful displays of all types of cakes. You chose by pointing to the cakes through the glass display and, one by one, the cakes were taken up with white gloves and placed in individual casings before they were arranged, four cakes per box, in a cardboard box that was assembled by the sales assistant and then tied with a string in a bow around the box so I could carry it home. A fantastic experience – but the value chain was too long and too expensive to scale, given the price of the cakes. No matter how much value the bakery added to the cakes, they could never charge enough to get the profit that they needed to expand. Unfortunately, the bakery did not survive; it closed when I was in my teens and I don't expect to see the likes of this again, at least not with the same value chain, or if I do the price will be so high only a small niche market will be able to afford it.

You must make your value proposition as great as possible while keeping the cost of delivery and the value chain in check so you can still make a profit. The hotel industry is a good example: getting the balance right between all the extra services the hotel could offer and still making a profit is a delicate balance. Often, new hotels offer more than they can afford to do in the longer term. I had a favorite guesthouse in the UK that I stayed in regularly, because it provided over-the-top service at an incredibly low price, but it did not last because the business simply could not make money. The proprietors were passionate about delivering great service but failed to watch the bottom line in the process.

Where is your focus in the value chain?

Understanding your own value chain will help you to understand the core of your value proposition: what can you do yourself very well and scale easily as you scale the business. It also tells you what is too difficult to do yourself in a new market or territory as you scale the business and so you must solve this problem without sacrificing your whole value proposition.

In one of my companies, DVM, we offered a digital media solution to mobile operators to allow them to market and sell premium content like games, music, ringtones and phone wallpaper pictures to their customers. This business had a very defined value chain: it was like a factory floor where the raw materials came in one door and the finished product went out the other door to the happy customers, assuming all went well in the process. In the early days, we did everything in-house: we took in raw content, processed it to make it fit all cell phones, loaded it to the retail store for the mobile operator, placed all the descriptions and prices on the display and then made sure that the product was delivered to the customers subject to payment. But this was a difficult proposition to scale because there was a very extended and protracted value chain involved in the delivery of the service to the customers. We needed to partner with people who specialized in the different parts of the value chain. So, for example, we partnered with a global company that could process all the raw content and deliver it to us in a finished product format for every device our customers had; we partnered with other companies that acted as aggregators and wholesalers of music to get all of the retailing data that was needed to showcase and retail the music track (photos, album and track details, etc.). Gradually, as the number of partners grew, we were able to focus on the core value of our proposition which was the technology that enabled the end-to-end value chain to source, retail and sell digital content using the partners to take responsibility for key bottlenecks in the value chain that we could do ourselves but in which we had no competitive advantage. In the end, we had a value proposition that we could scale and sell to any operator in any country without the need to hire a whole new team of people to replicate what we did in the early days in our office in the UK where we did everything in the value chain.

I met a CEO of a successful digital media company who decided many years ago that he wanted to continue to do all of the different aspects of the value chain in-house and sell directly to consumers. He told me much later that this decision was fundamentally wrong and that, if he had focused on developing the technology only and then allowing other partners to do all the other aspects of his value chain, he would have been able to export into new markets and accelerate the growth of his business. Instead, he was selling only in Ireland and had locked himself into an unscalable company that gave him a relatively modest income for a lot of hard work and would never be able to sell the business for a premium return on his life-long investment.

Your value proposition must be compelling to your customers

If you want to really accelerate the growth of your business your value proposition must be compelling to your target customers. This sounds so obvious that it hardly needs saying. But too many CEOs believe that their proposition is, or is not, compelling by definition and there is little or nothing that can be done about it; they believe that if you sell a product that is not compelling, then it is simply not compelling. I strongly believe that, no matter what you sell, you can make it compelling to your customers if you really understand what a value proposition looks like.

Some years ago, I knew the CEO of a company that was selling a generic technology into the telecoms industry, but it was up against lots of other companies that all sold the same product to the same industry with the same value proposition. The only difference was price – and this was being eroded by competition, so the business was heading for decline and not growth. The CEO struggled with what to do and, in the end, he decided to bring in a heavyweight Chief Marketing Officer (CMO) from a completely unrelated industry to see whether marketing could make the difference. After some months of looking at the product and the industry they were in, the new CMO decided that, although there were a lot of companies competing in the same market with the same proposition, there was no clear market leader. So he decided to create a market leader position by simply stating in all of the company's marketing communications that it was the number one company in this space. The company spent a lot of money on marketing to drive this message home; the objective was that everywhere one of their potential customers looked they saw this company positioned as the number one in the industry, not the cheapest but the best.

The strategy paid off. The company started to see growth after a just few months of the campaign and, in time, became the market leader, winning all the keynote speaker slots at all the main industry events. It was the authority on this industry and its customers were confident that when they bought from it they were choosing the market leader and would get the service they expected and the innovation that would come from a market leader. After a year or two of this, the company was acquired for nearly stg£200 million on a total investment of only stg£10 million. Needless to say, the investors were very pleased with the CEO who simply did not accept that his value proposition was not compelling.

The importance of perceived value

One thing to understand is the importance of perceived value: customers' perceptions of what they buy and what they get. If you get this wrong, you might have the most compelling proposition on paper but, because the customer perceives that the proposition is not compelling – or worse, it is perceived as more expensive than the competitors, then you are on a hiding to nothing.

Some time ago, a company approached me to get my feedback on a new cell phone offering in the market. The CEO told me that the value proposition was simple to understand in a world that is complicated (a good start): the company was offering a single price for all calls of 10 cents per minute. Research had shown that the average price that consumers were paying per minute for a call was closer to 20 cents, so the CEO believed this was a compelling proposition. The problem was that, at the time, consumers were buying unlimited call plans for topping up every 30 days, so the consumer had a perceived price per minute that was much lower than 20 cents, or even 10 cents. If you asked a consumer how much they paid per minute, they couldn't tell you but they didn't believe that 10 cents was good value. The company was wasting its money on trying to educate the market to this effect and could not break through with this value proposition. Consumers simply did not see it as compelling enough for them to change their current behavior, based on the perceived value of what they were getting already. The company ultimately failed.

7: Communicating Your Value Proposition to Your Customers

Understand your customer's constraints

When you are creating your value proposition, it is also important to understand the customer's own constraints.

Maybe they do not have the internal resources to integrate your new service, or the resources to sell it, etc. Once you know these constraints, you can solve these problems as part of your own value proposition. For example, in my own business today, Digital Trading where we sell Customer Relationship Engagement (CRE) software to mobile operators for their enterprise customers, we do all the work and offer a turnkey solution that does not require any integration into the operator's current infrastructure. If we did require such integration, then all the huge incumbent suppliers to the mobile operators would need to get involved and the project would get too slow, too expensive and too political. But knowing this allows us to work around it for the customer's benefit – and ours too! I was told by one of our customers that if we had not taken this approach, they would not have been able to buy our service.

Measure and prove your benefits

The more you can measure and prove the benefits to your customers, the more compelling you can make your value proposition and ultimately the business case for your target customer. For example, if you can state that your service is 50% cheaper than any of the competitors, that's a simple statement that customers can understand.

When I operated a cell phone service in Ireland called imagine, we simply told the customer that we were 20% cheaper than all the other operators. In doing so, we cut through the pricing complexity that all of the other operators were pushing into the market simply to confuse customers and to maximize their revenues. This worked for us because at the time the 20% discount was compelling; we won customers in large numbers and were very successful.

For bigger and more complex sales, you need to prepare the business case for your customer and show them that they can improves sales by x or reduce costs by y and that this means z in terms of the cash benefit to them. When you take this approach, you need to consider whether the pain for the customer or the benefit for them is big enough for them to change suppliers or to take on your new product or service. If it is not enough, then they may not care and you would be better served by moving on to a different customer where the pain / benefit ratio is big enough.

Competing with limited resources means listening to customers

One common concern from smaller companies that are trying to compete with much larger companies to supply similar products and services to the same customers is how they can compete with so little resources, less well-known brands, etc.

I have done this all throughout my career and today it never costs me a thought because I am so confident in the ability of a smaller company to compete effectively against a larger company if the small company really understand its value proposition. By listening very carefully to your customers, you always can find a problem to solve for them or an opportunity that can be exploited. The most important thing to do as a smaller company trying to win new customers, especially if they are larger and more complex customers, is to listen. I know this sounds obvious but you would be amazed at how many senior executives and salespeople cannot help themselves not listening to the customer. Many times, I have seen salespeople walk through every slide of their deck because they are so determined to get their pitch across as they want it heard by the customer. I once even witnessed the customer going asleep during the pitch!

Listening to the customer will tell you what issues they are trying to solve. You might focus just on a tiny piece of their problem for now but, by doing this, you could win a contract that allows you to grow into the customer over time. By doing an excellent job on the small issue, you can build trust with the customer and then they give you bigger challenges, etc.

If you are small, you will be expected to be innovative, agile and smart (as well as lower cost than the bigger suppliers). Again, use this to your advantage: tell customers all about your innovation but then come back to the practical problems that you can solve here and now. I have won many major contracts on the back of innovation, but then the service that they actually buy tends to be much more basic than the innovative service you were offering. Nonetheless, by winning the first small basic contract, you can grow into the larger offering.

Keep it simple, stupid!

Keep it simple, stupid! If you can get one single message across to the customer that they really understand and that can differentiate you from the other suppliers of your product or service, then that's enough. Don't confuse the customer with lots of messages.

For example, the iPhone does so many things that to list them all would only confuse the average customer. The key message that Apple got across to the average consumer was simplicity. Apple makes everything simple to find, simple to install and simple to use. Dyson, for example, got rid of the bag, without compromising on the performance of the vacuum cleaner, thus making it cheaper to operate after the customer bought it. innocent smoothies are made from totally natural ingredients. Ryanair is the low cost airline. What is your business known for or what would you like it to be known for in terms of your value proposition to your customer? Think about it and then communicate it clearly to the customer. The simpler and more compelling you can make this, the more powerful it will be for you as a tool to win customers.

How to capture your value proposition in your Accelerated Growth Plan slide deck ...

Your value proposition needs to capture, in a single sentence if possible, what the company does that is of value to your target customers.

Ideally, this value proposition should be easy for your customers to understand and be 'compelling' for them. If your value proposition will help your customers to increase their sales, put numbers on this – for example, "… will drive a 20% increase in sales." Your customers will understand and, if a 20% increase in sales is compelling for them, they will want to hear more or to buy your service.

Your value proposition should cover all the aspects of your product or service that customers value, including innovation, customer care, price, speed of delivery, the product/service itself, etc.

Try to differentiate your product/service from your competitors if possible in your value proposition statement. So to take the value proposition above, differentiate by adding "… but for 50% of the competition's cost."

My own company's value proposition is targeted at communications service providers and is "We offer an innovative Customer Relationship Engagement service, delivered over a Cloud under SaaS model, to help you win and retain high value enterprise customers and to drive more communications traffic over your network at higher prices."

Remember your value chain and be careful to highlight the value that your company brings. Be prepared to highlight other areas where you will work with partners or the customers themselves to complete the full value chain that allows you to scale the business. So, for example, I told mobile operators who were buying my digital media service that we worked with local content aggregators to deliver local content in local languages based on local customer demand. So it is clear what we do and what we don't do, but our service allows for the whole value chain; we could easily add the local content supplier using the technology we had built because we understood our value chain.

8

SIZING THE MARKET OPPORTUNITY

- Get your target market right
- Find a growth wave and ride it
- If you are in a declining market, redefine your market to achieve growth
- Know that markets disappear
- Don't always listen to the so-called market experts
- Find new opportunities in old markets
- Markets always change
- Markets move fast now
- Take account of partners / investors in defining your market
- Quantify your market
- Look for paradigm shifts

Your market opportunity is important because ...

This looks like stating the obvious but it's amazing how many companies cannot clearly identify or describe their target market – and even established companies that look like they have clearly identified and satisfied their market can get it badly wrong.

For example, when Ryanair was trying to break into the airline market, it struggled for a time because it defined the market as the existing customers of existing airlines. It was not until Ryanair decided to target the millions of people who at the time could not afford to travel by plane because air travel was seen as a luxury, for businesspeople and wealthy people, not for mass market consumers, that the company identified a new untapped market with huge demand. Ryanair now dominates this sector because it saw the market first and got a head start by building the company around this, using lower cost operations to service a lower cost market. These new untapped markets are sometimes called 'blue oceans', while competitive markets are known as 'red oceans.' The best blue oceans are usually sitting under our noses, very close to existing markets that we already serve.

I have attempted to create a new blue ocean market for Digital Trading by defining the market we operate in as CRE and not CRM, although the CRE market is very close to the CRM market. I believe that the CRE market is one that our CRM competitors have not yet seen. Smaller enterprises and smaller divisions within large enterprises do not understand and cannot use the complex CRM services that are offered today. They want something that offers easy-to-use two-way communications between their organization and their customers. I believe that, by creating a blue ocean for our service, we will accelerate the growth of the company way beyond what we could ever achieve if we competed in the same market as the dominant CRM players. In other words, this is our engine for accelerated growth.

Get your target market right

It is really important to understand the market that you are in, the customer you serve and how you serve them. This may sound obvious but I will give you some examples of what I mean.

I had the privilege of working with a great lady from the USA who helped large companies to define their strategy and the market that they targeted and served. One of her clients, which sold kitchen utensils for the household owner, had steadily declining sales as the younger generation who have faster lifestyles do less and less cooking in the home and prefer to eat out to save time. She suggested that the company was not in the business of selling pots and pans but in the business of helping its customer to cook a meal. These customers lived in large cities and had busy lifestyles, so the business needed a new strategy: to help its target customer to cook a meal. The company created a great online presence, full of free videos and materials on how to cook a simple meal in a short space of time – for example, impress your friends with a dinner party in your apartment with only 10 minutes' cooking needed. And – this was the clever part – here's the ideal pot or pan to use to do so. The new strategy was hugely successful and proves that, if you can get your market definition right and identify the target customer and their needs, you can grow a business even if you sell what looks like commodity products and services.

I worked with the CEO of another company that sold car parts online. It did a great job but needed to differentiate itself from the ever-increasing competition from other online retailers, so it focused their business on being "the car parts experts," a place where online customers for car parts could get information, tips, videos, etc. from a group of experts who knew everything there is to know about car parts. Through helping customers as the car parts experts, the business built up a loyal and regular base of repeat customers who see the value in what it offers over and above the competitors. Again, this has become the engine for growth, along with doing a great job at selling car parts online.

Find a growth wave and ride it

Markets come and go, it is their natural cycle: they emerge, grow, stay steady for a while and then contract as new markets emerge. Being able to identify these cycles is a key part of your company's success. If you can position your company to be ready to ride a growth wave, then you can be phenomenally successful just by being in the market when the growth comes.

In the early days of the cell phone market, growth was slow due to the cost of handsets, poor coverage and the high cost of calls, but when cell phones became affordable to the mass market, the market just took off – and when it did, everyone in the market, regardless of how good or bad they were, took off too. A number of companies that were in the cell phone market when it took off were hugely successful, just by being there, and their CEOs made a killing in the process. But some of these people who were hailed as heroes for the growth they achieved at that time have not been able to repeat their magic, because they believed that all of their success was due to their own skills and abilities as CEOs. To be very successful, you need both the skills as a CEO and the market wave to ride. It is not always possible to find a huge market wave that you can ride like the cell phone industry but there are always smaller waves that you can ride – or, if not, you can create your own wave like I did with the CRE industry.

If you are in a declining market, redefine your market to achieve growth

If you are stuck in a market that is no longer growing or is contracting, don't keep plodding along in the hope that something will change or that the market will come back. Get out of it – either by moving to a new market or by redefining the market that you operate in.

I worked with the CEO of a company that was in a market in decline, whose revenues also were in decline. We identified a market very similar to their current market that was already big and still growing. We carefully researched this new market to clearly identify the target customers and their needs that could be addressed by the company, using its existing products – to avoid the double risk of developing new products for a new market. Although it put him at risk of losing the support of his board – mainly VCs who were pushing for an exit – the CEO decided to pursue this strategy. He separated out some resources to address the new market while continuing to service his existing customers and maintaining the cash-flow needed to fund the diversification. He redefined the business through the company's website and sales materials while protecting sales to its existing customers. And he grew the business and got a successful exit to a larger company that wanted to address the new market opportunity that he had moved into.

Because he got it right in the end, he was a hero. But, if the diversification had not worked, almost certainly he would have been fired by his board. However, as the CEO of your business with the responsibility for accelerating the growth of the business, sometimes you need to make tough decisions, regardless of the feedback from your board and investors who may not be as close to the market as you are.

If you are stuck in a contracting market, you need to do something about it, while at the same time mitigating the risks of getting it wrong by protecting the current business and only risking what you can afford to lose until you have the evidence (in the form of actual sales) to support your move.

Know that markets disappear

Markets don't just contract and decline – they also disappear completely. Take for example the market for movie rentals: there was spectacular growth and profits as people rented video cassettes, which were replaced by DVDs, but today this physical rental market is disappearing as people move to buy all their digital content online. In a few years' time, our children will smile at the idea of us browsing around a retail store searching for music and movies to rent or buy!

I tried to work with a major video rental company to offer them an online video service, but the CEO refused to believe that the market for physical video would ever disappear and did not buy our service; the market did decline and his company is not trading any longer.

If you're in a market like this, you need to diversify – if necessary in parallel with your core physical market while you wait for the new market to evolve. If you don't, in time your business will not exist. Some CEOs of more traditional businesses that have been around for years argue that their company has been through tougher times and survived and eventually grown. But I would counter argue that the market we operate in today involves different business models and markets that simply disappear all together, unlike many years ago when markets for products and services had a much longer life cycle and were simpler to understand and predict. Could a PC-maker have predicted the recent overwhelming switch by consumers from PCs to tablets, given that tablets had been in the market for years? It was the simplicity of use introduced by Apple's iPad that drove the masses to this new market; now the PC market is in rapid decline.

Don't always listen to the so-called market experts

When it comes to markets, you need to use commonsense, not listen to the so-called experts – because they often get it badly wrong.

I remember having heated debates with potential investors in my digital media business, which was based on people paying for digital content such as music, games and videos using their cell phones. The experts quoted market research that proved the trend towards people taking digital content for free from the Internet; therefore, they said, there would be a much smaller market for premium digital content over time. I argued that people would pay happily for the digital content they used if they could find it, buy it and use it in a simple and easy-to-use way. Again and again, I lost the argument because the experts had the research evidence to prove me wrong – but look at iTunes, the iPhone and the market today for paid digital content, which continues to grow because it is now simple to use. The vast majority of consumers in the market are happy to pay for a good service if it is simple to access and use – most will not take the trouble to search for free content on the Internet.

Find new opportunities in old markets

As markets move, there are always ways to exploit new opportunities in the old market. In music, for example, people can get mainstream music for free or for a tiny cost. So instead of everything riding on the back of selling a mass-market studio-produced perfect quality music track, the industry should move to selling music experiences to people who are passionate about certain music and artists. Real fans want more unique and specific content – and they will pay more for it. For example, concert tickets continue to sell as artists create unique and exciting experiences for their fans and outtakes from the studio where the artists are just chatting about general stuff are some of the most valuable content in the market today for older bands.

Digital Trading is a good example of this; we are selling our service to communication service providers (CSPs) that have sold traditional communications services to their customers for many years. We are helping them to sell new types of communications services to their existing customers. Often the customers are focused on the single type of communication that they continue to purchase from the CSP but, by adding some value to this, using our technology and simplicity of use, over time we will upsell more of our communications services to these customers as they see the benefits. This is finding new opportunities in old markets and then redefining the market on the way.

Markets always change

Markets constantly shift, changing to new forms that require companies to evolve.

Software is a good example: once upon a time, software was sold for a once-off license fee – a profitable and cash-generative arrangement for software providers. Then, as budgets got tight, the business model changed to offering a monthly fee-based managed service. Then it changed again to offering the software as a service where the customer only pays as they use the software – the software as a service (SaaS) model. And we are seeing the market shift again to a freemium model, where most of the software features are offered free to the customer but, if they want to do more, they need to upgrade to a premium paid version – look at Skype or Dropbox.

Another example of a market that is changing dramatically or that is about to change dramatically is banking. Some years ago, when I needed additional income, I applied for a job as a director on the board of one of the Irish banks. The job description asked for someone with a different perspective and a background in technology and innovation – so I thought "Why not?" I got called to an interview with the board – what an interesting conversation. The directors asked me where I saw the future of banking going. I said that banking services would go online as the primary interface to customers, cash would continue to disappear from our lives and bricks and mortar branch offices would be less and less important to customers based on our busy lifestyles.

What would be important would be the customer's relationship with his/her key account manager, which could be maintained largely over the phone or online. The directors dismissed my ideas out of hand and reiterated the importance of retail outlets, stating that online banking would never catch on. Needless to say, I did not get the job. But today banks are being forced to move in this direction to take costs out of the business – those that do it well (not just by cutting costs but by adding value for customers) will lead the market and win new customers in a market that is very competitive due to the regulatory restrictions on entry; those that don't make the changes will fail.

Markets move fast now

Business life cycles are now shorter, which means you need to move faster and be sure about the market you are operating in and the potential trends in it in order to maximize your growth potential.

When you are looking at a market, observe trends. In particular, if you are focused on consumer markets, look at consumers' lifestyles as they are today and where are they going as the world evolves. Today, with the globalization of technology and access to markets, markets can come and go in a much shorter space of time. Certainly, if you are operating in technology markets, new players can come in and dominate very quickly if they get it right and other players then are left fighting for survival.

Take account of partners / investors in defining your market

While getting your market definition right is critical for your success, it's also important in terms of bringing in serious partners or raising significant funding.

Clearly, you need to know your market very well; you also need to be able to identify trends, both positive and negative, that will impact your business and then explain how you will capitalize on a particular market dynamic.

In addition, you need to take into account your partners'/investors' perceptions of your market. If there is a bad sentiment around the particular market in which you have positioned your company, then you may need to change the market you are in and shift your products and service to another market that is close to your current market – or risk losing the support you need to accelerate your company's growth.

A lot of investors got badly burnt in the telecoms market and, as a result, many of them will not even look at an investment that sells services to the telecoms market. I disagree with this thinking and argue that, when markets change dramatically, huge opportunities emerge for new players that can spot them. But I am not going to convince these investors to take another look at this market until they see the huge opportunities and rewards that can be achieved by working in these markets now, when many others have turned their backs on them. VCs and investors can be a bit like farmers who all move to the markets that made money last year, but inevitably rarely make any money because everyone has moved to the same market at the same time. To make real money, you often need to go in the opposite direction to the market-followers.

Quantify your market

As part of your growth plan, you need to be able to quantify your market and measure it – either from the top down or from the bottom up. The way you measure it will depend on how big the market is and how easy it is to quantify.

For example, if you are selling cell phone handsets into a market, you can buy a report that quantifies the size of the market by country, by region and by operator and device types. Often, there is an endless choice of reports created by well-known research companies. You then can quote the numbers to any potential business partner, and use the report to target key sub-markets that best fit your business growth objectives. This is the top-down approach: take the numbers for the whole market and then work your way down to the numbers that you are setting out to achieve as a share of the market that you can win. But be careful with this approach and don't be tempted to quote unrealistic numbers or ambitions. For example, stating that all you need to do is win 1% of the global mobile subscriber market means very little to potential investors and partners – you need to be able to prove how you will do it.

Describing a market from the bottom up often is more compelling. Take a business case for a single typical customer and then describe the size of the market based on winning x more of these customers in your home market, market number two, etc. – in other words, you build up your market size based on hard facts for the customers you already have.

Using both the top-down and bottom-up approaches in combination provides a powerful and convincing understanding of your market, not just for external partners but also for internal planning and setting growth expectations. Watch the professional do the mental math for your market. A good VC will tell you quickly what they think of the market you are in and how good your plan is relative to the potential market. People talk a lot about VCs investing in the founder, but one of the most important investment criteria for a VC is the market potential for the business – unless it is operating in a market that has huge growth potential, they just walk away.

8: Sizing the Market Opportunity

But a word of caution: VCs are not always right. I remember discussing the potential market for digital music in Nigeria with investors. Many of them simply concluded that there was no market because all music sold in Nigeria at the time was bootlegged, the major music labels having pulled out of the market completely in the belief that there was no market worth having. But we persisted and ultimately deployed a music service with MTN, the largest mobile operator in Nigeria. I won't pretend it was a runaway success but there was a market for digital music where customers would pay if the service was easy to access and easy to use – and it's still growing today.

Look for paradigm shifts

As part of the market discussion, you also need to be able to describe the market opportunity: something is broken, huge gap, enormous growth, significant shift, or better still a paradigm shift in the market.

I worked with one investor whose key criterion for investment was a potential paradigm shift in the market. In his experience, companies that saw the shift coming and were prepared to capitalize on it could grow very fast and become very successful in a very short space of time, taking a market leader position that ultimately led to their acquisition by bigger companies that did not see the shift coming or could not respond fast enough.

How to capture your market opportunity in your Accelerated Growth Plan slide deck ...

In your slide, explain your target market by:

- **Defining the target market:** Your initial target market may be your market 'sweet spot' of customers you can target and win easily – where do you go from there? You may address one market sector to prove out your product or service, before widening into other market sectors;
- **Indicate the size of the market:** Bottom-up, top-down or both;
- **Talk through a typical customer's buying pattern:** This gives credibility to the sizing and is evidence of the existence of the market; the more real customers that you can refer to with the same requirements, the more credibility your market sizing will have;
- **State the market dynamics:** Is it growing? How fast? How/why will this growth be sustained in the long term? Be careful not to show a market that is too big and out of reach, or too small and not exciting enough; make it real and compelling but easy to reach.

Show markets using maps and diagrams. For example, if your service is a subset of a much bigger market, then show it on a pie chart; if you plan on entering a small market to start with before expanding to a wider market, then show this as layers in circles. Help the audience to visualize the market and your approach to it.

9

WHAT PROBLEM DO YOU SOLVE FOR YOUR CUSTOMERS?

- Speak in a language the customer understands
- Customers only take small steps – not giant leaps
- Customers don't do complicated
- Keep it simple
- Focus on the benefits, not the features
- Don't add features just because you can
- You must give customers a compelling reason to change their behavior
- Keep iterating your product or service based on customer feedback

Your solution to your customer's problem is important because ...

Assuming you have explored and understand your value proposition to your customers, then the next step is how to deliver this to the customer: what does the product or service look and feel like or what is the customer experience?

If your value proposition is a product with excellent customer support, consider this example. I bought my first Bose stereo system second-hand from a friend some years ago. I used it for about 10 years and then, when I moved house, I put it in storage. When I took it out of storage and switched it on, it did not work. My immediate reaction was panic: how will I be able to afford to get this fixed since I cannot afford to buy a new one, OMG I will be without a sound system in the house (in my house, this is like having no running water). So I found the customer support number for Bose and phoned them. They took all the details of the now 13-year-old stereo and told me that I would receive a large envelope in the post in a few days: just package up the stereo, seal the box, place the sticker from the envelope on the box and call the number on the sticker for a courier to collect it. I asked the person on the call for an estimate of the cost of the work before they did anything, but she insisted that I should not worry about this, and that they would call before they incurred any cost for me. A few weeks passed and UPS delivered a box to me from Bose. I assumed it was Bose returning my stereo with an estimate or, worse, telling me they could not fix it due to its age, but when I opened the box there was a letter on top that read: "Dear Mr Dowling, As you are a valued customer of Bose, we have completely refurbished your stereo unit. We have installed the latest software and it is now working as good as new. We hope you enjoy using our products for many more years to come. There is no charge for this service." Talk about being bowled over as a customer. I was already a fan of their products but having experienced the full service wrap-around – their value proposition – I am now a diehard customer and an advocate for life!

As a CEO, if you really want to accelerate the growth of your business, you need to get the total experience perfect for the customer.

Speak in a language the customer understands

When you are selling to consumers, it is very important to speak their language, to make sure that your messages are understood and that the customer knows why they should buy your products. In the technology world, companies get this wrong all the time. They invent a great technology and then forget how to communicate this to their customers. Some companies focus entirely on the product – not on the benefits.

As an example, in the broadband world simply tell the customer that your broadband service is 10 times faster than any other provider in the market. They don't care about the technology that delivers the improvement. All they want is a faster service at a good price – so focus on that as the key message.

Customers only take small steps – not giant leaps

Innovative entrepreneurs come up with the most visionary ideas, often creating products or services light years away from where the market is today. But consumers only take small steps – not giant leaps. If your business is engaged in real innovation that leads the market, it will cost a lot of money to educate the market and to get mass consumers to adopt your new product/service – hence the phrase: 'leading edge, bleeding edge.' A safer bet to achieve mass-market adoption is to help customers to improve their current experience significantly without having to make noticeable changes to their current behavior.

I have learned this lesson the hard way. In one of my companies, the investors had ploughed a lot of money into a product that offered the mass-market consumer a completely automated personal assistant that would answer the phone and direct the call to any of your numbers: home, mobile, office, etc; it could take messages and receive faxes; and it talked the caller through every step of the process. It was just amazing technology that had the potential to revolutionize the way people used communications services at the time. But, great technology does not mean a great service. We implemented the product in a trial environment and, after a few weeks of using the service myself, my wife came on the phone to me and in fairly robust language told me to get rid of it because it was driving her crazy. Before this, she just called my mobile, it rang and I answered immediately or, if I was unavailable, she left a message and I called her back, but now she had to wait for ages while the automated personal assistant called number after number to find me. It was a very bad experience for the caller. I realized then that the product would fail in the market, but the investors insisted that we launch it. I refused to do the public launch and left the investors run with it on their own, which they did to great fanfare. Needless to say, it did not succeed; maybe some day the market will be ready for it.

You need to make sure that your products and services are easy-to-use and add real benefit. You cannot expect customers to change their current behavior unless there is both a compelling reason and an easy way to do so. It is always better to work with what the customer is already familiar with and integrate this in providing your new product/service. Look at how Facebook can integrate to other services, or your contacts in Outlook can be automatically synchronized with Skype or LinkedIn.

Customers don't do complicated

Text messages – the SMS that we know today – came to the market almost by accident, but they were so simple to use and so powerful that consumers adopted them *en masse*. But the technology was already there in most of the networks, the investment to roll out the service was very low relative to the revenues it generated, and so the cell phone operators made billions in profits.

Then came multimedia messaging (MMS), which allowed a consumer to create and send a multimedia file continuing pictures, sound and text. Operators bailed into this new technology and invested millions in buying and deploying it for consumers to upgrade to it. To recover the additional investment, operators typically charged four times as much for an MMS as an SMS because of the value they believed it provided to customers. But consumers did not adopt the technology, for the simple reason that it was too complicated and too expensive. Today, you can send pictures and messages very simply from an iPhone free of charge or through apps like Whatsapp or Viber – as a result, consumers are starting to use this technology but no one is paying for it, it is free.

I have fallen foul of this advice myself. Some years ago, I pitched an innovative and complex proposition to a mobile operator in Sri Lanka. They wanted to work with us but kept telling us that our service was too complicated for their market. In the end, they went with a different supplier who delivered a dial-up premium voice service offering weather information, news and ringtones. The service was a huge success and generated millions of dollars for both the supplier and the operator. We easily could have delivered this simpler solution but I must admit that I turned my nose up at this business because it was so basic and we could do so much more. I would not walk away from this business today: I would deliver the service that they wanted, no matter how basic and, over time, I would migrate the customers to more advanced services as a step-by-step process while generating good revenues at every stage of the process.

Don't be too proud if you want to grow revenues and ultimately grow your business. Look at the thousands of businesses that sell very basic and uncomplicated products and services to consumers all over the world. They generate a lot of sales and make a lot of profit in the process. Many of them talk about innovation but still they focus on the core offerings that generate revenues today with a view to gradually migrating customers to their more innovative products as they come to market on a phased step-by-step roadmap.

Keep it simple

Simplicity is a golden rule for scaling your business. It needs to be applied at every touchpoint for all of your customers.

In online retailing, the power of simplicity becomes a very stark and measurable component of the business. Helping customers to find the products and services they want to buy, quickly and easily, is the first step; the next step is helping them to check out and pay, again quickly and easily. The number of clicks or data collection fields that you put in place has a direct correlation with the number of customers who abandon the process; every extra click makes a customer walk away without finishing their purchase.

I experienced this first-hand when we deployed a content purchase solution to a European mobile operator. A few months after launch, the operator's parent company insisted on a higher level of security for customer purchases: instead of a one-click purchase process where the content was billed to the customer's cell phone bill, the customer now had to input a PIN number for every purchase. When we implemented this, sales plummeted. Customers saw this as an extra step that made the purchase too complicated to be bothered with.

Focus on the benefits, not the features

If you track the exponential growth in the sale of cell phones, you will see that the big sellers always focused on key benefits to the consumer and not on the technology features which have continued to grow at a rate that makes it too difficult to list all of them.

My first cell phone was nearly as big as a car battery with a wired phone attached. This was supposed to be mobile – that is, you carried it around with you all day – so the key benefit in the early days was size: the smaller the phone, the more sales. As the size reduced, the next problem was the aerial, which still protruded from the phone. Mitsubishi created a phone with a retractable aerial, before aerials became integrated into the phone body itself. The next problem was battery life: as the battery life increased, the sales increased. Nokia cracked this to the extent that you did not think about it any more: a battery charge would last for days, until the new smartphones came along. If you could offer an iPhone that had a battery life that lasted several days, it would be a big hit again.

I met the founders of Bluetooth (Cambridge Silicon Radio) who described how difficult it was in the early days to sell their technology, until the government decided that it was safer if people did not use a handheld phone in their car. Bluetooth technology took off, not because of the features of the technology but because of the safety benefits while driving a car; and the legislation prohibiting handheld phones in cars was the icing on the cake for the company to massively accelerate its growth.

Another example is the video rental market: the key benefit for me to use an online video rental service is not having to go to a retail store in town to pick out the video and, more importantly, not having to repeat the process to get it back on a Monday morning.

Don't add features just because you can

I am driving home the point about keeping things simple for your customers because it is such a critical factor for accelerated growth.

I was asked by the CEO of a large division of a very large global organization to review a new technology that the company was developing for the home. The product was amazing: it could manage the household budgets, arrange the family calendar of events and send out reminders, order food from a supermarket, etc. All great stuff but it made no sense to the customer: apart from it being overly complicated to use, customers would have to give up their existing calendars, contacts lists, home phone, etc. Instead of integrating and working with what customers were already used to, this company expected customers to change all of their products for this one 'super-product'. The company had the budget to develop the 'super-product', which potentially allowed it to dominate the market for many different types of service. I told the CEO that this was a bridge too far and that it would never work. Because of the significant investment of people and cash that had already gone into developing this product, the company was not able to kill it. So it came to market with a very low profile and failed; consumers simply did not want to adopt it.

You must give customers a compelling reason to change their behavior

If a product or service requires the customer to change their behavior, this is difficult to achieve no matter how brilliant the product or service: people like what they are used to. To get people to change their behavior, you need to give them a compelling reason to do so.

In Digital Trading, we are bringing our new CRE service to enterprises that have never used any type of CRM before, so we are asking them to change their behavior. Take for example restaurants, which typically use a paper diary for customer bookings. If customers fail to show on the day of the booking, there is a significant cost to the restaurant. So we focus on the problem and highlight that, if they use our CRE service, it automatically will send an SMS to remind the customer of the booking so that the customer can respond and confirm. If this catches even just one potential missed booking, it prevents the restaurant losing the revenue from the booking, which could be worth hundreds of euro when compared to the 6 cents they would pay us for the SMS.

A great example of how people have changed their behavior *en masse* is the cell phone. Today, virtually everyone in the developed world has a cell phone and it is hard to imagine what life was like before we had them. But not too long ago, when the cell phone first arrived in the market, I used to sell them to senior executives of large enterprises. If I was lucky, I would sell one phone per month – in a good month, maybe two. The typical response from the customer was "Why do I need a cell phone when I have a phone on my desk and one at home?"

And I remember one evening visiting an old aunt of mine and bringing my cell phone; it was the first time that she had seen one of them. While I was there, the cell phone rang and I answered it. The next day, my mother called me to say that my aunt thought it was very rude to bring a cell phone into her house and to answer a call. I replied to my mother that my aunt did not take her phone off the hook when I arrived and she also took a call while I was there. The difference was a change of behavior.

Keep iterating your product or service based on customer feedback

I am a great believer in designing a product or service by starting with customer feedback, using slides or prototypes. When I designed my Nautique aftershave, I spent weeks on the streets of Dublin asking potential customers to pick out their favorite smell, then their favorite packaging, etc. I kept tweaking the product until we got it right.

I do the same today with technology. Typically, we show the potential customer screenshots of the service to get their feedback. Then we create a prototype demo based on the feedback and show it to more customers. Based on this feedback, we start to design the finished product/service but again, when we deliver it to a live customer, we continue to gather their feedback and continue to iterate the product. We continue this process until the customers are completely happy that the product is simple to use and has all the key features and benefits that they need today with more to come tomorrow. (Agile programming uses the same iterative process.)

In Digital Trading, we have spent a number of years developing and perfecting our CRE product to make it so simple to use that a new user does not need any assistance; they instinctively know how to use it from first sign-on. This is a critical factor for scaling the business, particularly when you add in the need for most of our customers to change their behavior.

How to capture your solution to your customer's problem in your Accelerated Growth Plan slide deck ...

In one slide if possible, talk about the problem in the market that your target customers have and how you solve it in a compelling way that makes them buy.

The next slide is your solution: a description of your product or service. It is important to ensure that your audience understands exactly what you do based on this slide (or a few slides if necessary).

When doing a pitch to investors, often it is useful to tell them upfront what you do. Only proceed with the rest of your pitch when you are sure that everyone has a clear understanding of what you do. Repeatedly, VCs complain about pitches where, by the end, they still have no idea what the business does; this is a fundamental error in pitching that should never happen. So make sure what you do is obvious to all early in your presentation.

If it is not feasible to do demos, then screenshots or photos of your product or service are the next best thing. Use cartoons or moving images where possible to show more complex products or services. But whatever you do, make sure they understand exactly what you do and how you do it.

10

COMMUNICATING YOUR MESSAGE TO THE MARKET

- The importance of branding
- You can build a brand by association
- Believe in your own brand
- Build a brand but use direct response marketing to sell
- In B2B, it pays to be a market leader
- Do your market research
- Guerrilla marketing is very cost-effective
- Sponsorship works if you get the right event
- Testimonials are powerful marketing tools

Your marketing is important because ...

Marketing and sales are often linked because it can be difficult to distinguish one from the other in terms of winning customers: you need good marketing to win new customers but you also need to be good at sales to close the deal. Getting both right is critical for scaling any business.

Marketing is a key tool available to you as CEO to accelerate the growth of your business but only the best companies really leverage its power. Marketing spans many different facets, from brochures to advertisements to entertainment events for customers but, if you are good at marketing, it will span every aspect of the business and be part of the culture of your organization.

Marketing is one of the most underused weapons available to companies that want to accelerate their growth, often because its potency is less well-understood by senior executives of mid-sized companies. A classic example of how a company stepped out from the crowd through great marketing is innocent, the smoothies company. There were hundreds of companies creating good smoothies already in the market but, from the outset, innocent followed a strategy of building a brand around quality and creating mass-market awareness for its products to drive them off the shelf. Yes, this strategy costs a lot of money and can be high-risk – but get it right (as innocent did) and the rewards are enormous. Apart from higher sales, your company becomes more valuable if you have a brand that is recognized in the market.

The importance of branding

To me, a brand is the representation of your business: your logo, brochures and documents should all look and feel like there is a core brand at work in the business. By getting this right, you can communicate quality and trust that is picked up both internally by your own staff and externally by anyone who touches your business.

When I was in my early 20s, I set up an accountancy practice in my home town of Carlow. It came from my desire to act as a consultant to many different businesses to get a feel for the industry that I would choose for my business and entrepreneurial career ahead. I started with one or two customers based on friends and family but I knew that, to scale the business and ultimately build value in it, so that I could sell it to a third party, I needed to build a brand. The brand needed to show a mature business with lots of history, a safe pair of hands coming from an accountancy background. My letterheads and brochures were important but I could not achieve the brand effect from these alone, so I looked at old buildings in Carlow town until someone pointed me to the old railway station. The station-master's old house, a beautiful building built in the

1800s, was perfect for an office and, because no one could see its potential, I got it for little or no rent. I took it over and renovated it to look like a very old office by installing old wood panels on the walls etc. This building had a huge impact on growing the business quickly: I remember after winning a large contract, the owner of the business said to me, "You must consider yourself very lucky to have inherited such an old and well-established practice from your father." Just the brand effect I was looking for!

You can build a brand by association

If budgets are scarce, you can build a brand by association.

I used this tactic very effectively when I was trying to build my Nautique aftershave brand. I had no money to spend on advertising, yet I wanted to compete with the big brands like Boss, Polo, etc. So I made sure that my product was positioned on the same shelf as these products and priced at the same price point with a product that was equal, if not better, in every respect. This strategy was hugely successful for building an unknown brand with no budget.

I did the same with iO by displaying our content partners' brands – companies like Sony, EMI, Discovery, Disney, etc. – so we could gain instant credibility in the market as a key supplier with substance.

Believe in your own brand

Brand values are what you stand for – although many brands say the same things, branding matters and works to help a company accelerate its growth. I am a great believer in getting everyone to buy into the company brand, its products and its culture. For example, when we created the imagine brand, we gave everyone a baseball cap with the logo, I wore a jacket that had the logo on it in bold writing, and we created brochures and information leaflets that looked cool. We infused the brand and what it stood for into the organization. This works; when your own people start to believe in a brand, they will live it and they carry the brand values into customer meetings, marketing meetings, supplier meetings, etc.

I engaged with a major US company that was looking to acquire an Irish technology company. During the acquisition, the US CEO commented, "When we buy a company, we make sure that we send two branded T-shirts to the employee's home – one for them and one for their partner – to make sure that they know they are now part of our team and to let their partners know also." I smiled at the thought of this being important enough to the CEO for him to say it in the midst of a deal worth millions of dollars, but he was right: it matters.

Build a brand but use direct response marketing to sell

I have always used marketing to my advantage. However, although it is one of the most powerful business tools available to business managers, it is always difficult to get the balance right in terms of what you do, how much you spend and getting the results. That's why I am a great believer in direct response advertising, which means you advertise a call-to-action and expect an immediate response from the customers. Brand advertising is much softer, more expensive and less measurable, though the sheer might of brand spend can drive through even the most mundane product.

When we created imagine we deliberately wanted to break away from the background that was mobile technology created by techies but used by consumers, so we were one of the first companies in the mobile business to create a totally consumer-focused brand: "imagine and anything is possible" was our strapline. It was very effective and cut through the other operators' millions of euros of advertising in the Irish market at the time and got us results. In particular we used direct response advertising, which had not been done in any significant way in mobile before: we ran ads on TV and radio that said "Dial this number now to get 20% off your cell phone bill." When we first went out with this advertising we had about 10 people in a call center waiting to take the calls; we found we needed significantly more to handle the volume of calls – actually, the switchboard blew up due to the response to the first ad and so we had to pull the ads temporarily. In the end, we found we could only snatch calls when the ads ran on TV; then we would call back the customer when the panic died down and walk them through the sign-up process.

When I went into Meteor to take over the sales and marketing function, the company was spending a fortune on building the brand – really funny ads on the TV but no product information and no call-to-action. So I switched the spend to product advertising with a call to action, keeping only a small amount for brand advertising. We went out with ads that told people the price of the phone, the service we offered and where to get it. We did a direct response ad campaign offering free SIM cards: the offer was €100 of free call credits, but they needed to top up by €10 each month to get another €10 for the 10 months to make up the €100. This was a huge success and brought the average cost of acquisition down from over €200 per customer to less than €65, while generating good monthly revenues from the customers that stayed.

When you get direct response right, it's like a sausage machine: when you need more sausages, you turn on the machine. You get people to respond by offering them something compelling; then you make it easy for them to respond so they do it now; and last you close the deal and get customers activated and spending money. You end up with a process that becomes predictable with a clearly defined cost of acquisition that gets built into the overall costs associated with your service.

In B2B, it pays to be a market leader

Advertising to another business – B2B – sometimes is a little different but your objectives are the same: you want to create awareness and confidence in your product or service and ultimately to get new customers. Taking a market leadership role is a good place to be in B2B. If you have something innovative or something to say about a particular industry you can set yourself up to become the market spokesperson, thus getting speaker slots at conferences, news articles for the related topic, etc. You can do all of this on a budget, but you need to plan it and make it happen by putting out key messages, doing things a little differently, etc.

In iO we were trying to get the attention of much larger players, so we targeted the industry conferences. We could not afford to sponsor events or take speaker slots, so we came up with the idea of speed-dating-type lunches where attendees got to meet someone interesting from the industry to learn something new; as the lunch went on, you moved table to meet someone else. This was new: before this, people would just sit wherever and have their lunch and by chance they might meet someone, but now the conference organizer could charge more for the lunch, give a better experience and give the attendee the opportunity to meet someone specific that made their trip more valuable to the company they worked for. It worked and, because we brought it to the conference organizers, we got a key role in every lunch free of charge. As we made a name for doing this, we got more invites – again, free.

Getting your first speaker slot at an industry conference can have the same effect. If you give a good speech, make it interesting for the audience and get good feedback from attendees, the organizers will ask you back again and again free of charge. But this rarely happens by chance; you may need to pay for the first speaker slot, but if you are good you might get called again free.

Do your market research

Before you bet your shirt on your marketing, make sure you have done your research. Every book you read about creating a business plan or starting your own business talks about this but many CEOs do not listen to the advice. If you are planning on accelerating the growth of your business and you are planning to use marketing as one of your key strategic initiatives, make sure you know (really know) your customers, your target market, your value proposition and what makes it compelling, your call to action and the associated P&L that makes it all add up at the end of the day.

It took me three years of market research to start building my current product and then another two years to get it right. Looking at it today, you would say it is simple – but simplicity is difficult to achieve without lots of research, refining and more research. The same goes for marketing: you need to get right the target audience, the communications message, the media you use and the experience you expect your customer to have when they try your product.

Many companies employ market research agencies to conduct this market research. I learned the hard way that this can be a very expensive and often useless exercise. I much prefer to do my own market research: whenever possible, sit in on customer interviews; allow free-flowing questions and answers, not tick-the-box surveys; let the customers comment about anything they like; but, best of all, talk to customers yourself.

Guerrilla marketing is very cost-effective

Some of the best marketing I ever did was in imagine, where we had very small budgets and were up against giants like Vodafone and O2, so we had to do a lot of guerrilla marketing. This is where you set out to steal an event from another advertiser by doing something dramatic that takes all the publicity away from them and over to you.

One of the best instances of this was at a major concert in Slane Castle, where Vodafone was the main sponsor. They had a row of new jeeps, all fully branded and being driven by models; we bought very old Minis, painted them as imagine (the 'Italian Job' look) and used very good looking girls but with attitude. When our Minis arrived at the concert, uninvited, they drove past the Vodafone jeeps that were lined up outside the venue and went up to the gates of the venue. The organizers thought they looked so cute that they let them in and our girls drove around the concert venue giving out free toys with imagine branding. After the event, one of the Minis was escorted by a policeman through the front doors of a pub in the local town – for which we got front-page press coverage. This is guerrilla marketing at its best.

Sponsorship works if you get the right event

Sponsorship of a great event can give you good value for money in terms of brand advertising. One example was when Meteor launched: we got a deal to sponsor the Irish Music Awards (later to be called the Meteor Music Awards). In the first year, the big attraction was U2. Although we did not know whether they would come until the last minute, they did and the event became a huge success for a modest spend. And the fun we had in the VIP private party after the concert gave us work experiences to remember forever.

Testimonials are powerful marketing tools

If you are working with a small budget, one of the most successful marketing tools is customer testimonials, telling everyone how great your product or service is. It can be very compelling for other new customers to hear how successful your service has been for them. Testimonials are cheap – often free – and easy to publish online or to embed into a PowerPoint presentation.

If you have a bigger product or service that has a long sale cycle, a great way to get new customers is to select a reference customer that potential new customers can visit or talk to, where your service is making a compelling difference. Even if you make no real money from this customer, the problems you solve for them are proof to other customers that your product/service works.

I used Manx Telecom as our reference customer for iO. Manx was tiny relative to other mobile operators but was an excellent reference customer because it had all the latest network technology and a great CEO who was happy to host visits to showcase the company's innovation with partners like us.

How to capture your marketing in your Accelerated Growth Plan slide deck ...

In your slide on marketing, try to explain how you propose to get your brand and your product awareness into the target market. Define this target market and how you can reach it in the most cost-effective way. Then focus on how you will get sales results, the cost of acquisition, the sale process and the delivery of the service to the customer to make sure you close the sales loop.

11

ACHIEVING YOUR SALES TARGETS

- Good salespeople are hard to find
- Choose your salespeople carefully
- Get your sales presentation right
- Focus on winning strategic customers
- Build a predictable sales pipeline
- Make sure the basic selling skills are being applied
- Make sure all the decision-makers are on board
- Learn to say "No"
- Saying "No" can produce some incredible results
- Talk to your customers and listen
- Thank your customers – personally
- Build relationships with your customers
- Make your sales effort scalable through partners
- Be careful what you wish for

Your sales are important because ...

Achieving sales is the single most important activity in any business. It is the life blood that pulses through every vein. Without sales, the business simply will fail. I know this is obvious but yet it never ceases to amaze me the number of business plans that I have seen in my career where forecasts for sales are dramatically off, while forecasts for overheads and costs are fantastically accurate.

The easiest part of any business to predict and control is how much money you will spend, because you are in control of this. If you hire 10 people, you know exactly what you will pay for salaries, office space and equipment, etc. But sales are not predictable; you don't have the same level of control over winning new customers and receiving the cash, since customers have the final say in buying your products and services.

Therefore, it is critical to focus your efforts on sales and only to build your costs based on these sales. If you can do this, you will build a very strong and profitable business – in accounting terms, this is called the zero plus approach: you start with zero costs and build as you need to.

In my current business, I have chosen to make my entire costs variable: engineers to build the product, operations people to support it, sales people to help sell, all are variable costs that I switch on only when they are absolutely necessary and switch off when they are not. This allows me to stretch my cash to last longer. Later, as sales come in, I can start to incur the fixed costs of permanent staff and offices, etc.

Good salespeople are hard to find

Sales often can be elusive: new start-ups sometimes never get a customer for their products and ultimately fail; established companies can struggle to get new sales if the market has slowed or competitors have eaten away market share. Selling is the most complex activity in your organization and requires the most focus and skills but it is often the most ignored, most under-resourced and under-skilled activity in a business. In your own business, how many people work in sales? Are they your best people? Are they highly qualified for the job?

Salespeople are often the least skilled in any organization. For such an important role, it is amazing how little training or professional skills are associated with sales; most of the salespeople you meet just decided to be in sales and have learned their skills, or lack of skills, on the job. This role is critical to the success of a business and yet there are few formal qualifications or schools that focus on training sales executives in the same way that we produce engineers, accountants, HR executives, marketing people, etc.

The other problem is that sales people usually are very good at selling themselves. So, often, you buy the blurb and then later realize you have made a mistake. It is so important to check references for salespeople, and not just the references that they volunteer to you, which are usually from their best friends. Check the ones they don't offer up; check their previous employment and the great sales figures they produced in the past, making sure they owned the sale and not someone else. Did they get paid the commission? Did they lead the sale? Did they close it?

If you get your sales hiring wrong, you have blown the most important resource of the business at a critical time when the business needs new sales to scale; this can be enough to bring the business down, especially when you have long sales cycles.

Having said all this, it is possible to find really good salespeople. When you do, look after them well, because they can keep delivering over and over again and the business can accelerate its growth through their efforts.

I have no problem with successful salespeople being the highest paid people in the business; it is a tough job and, as long as the business benefits from new sales and each sale contributes to the bottom line, then why not share the rewards with the successful salespeople? If other people in your organization complain, as they often do in these circumstances, then let them become a salesperson and get the same deal.

Choose your salespeople carefully

To accelerate the growth of your business, getting the right salespeople into your organization is very important. It takes time and effort to get this right. But what makes a successful salesperson and what should you look out for? My own experience suggests:

- **Building relationships with customers in today's market is very important:** You need to see this ability in your salespeople. The test is whether you would enjoy their company. Would you spend an evening with them and not talk shop? If you don't like spending time with your salespeople, how do you expect your customers to do so?
- **Are your salespeople passionate about what they do and how they do it?** Believe it or not, there are lots of excellent salespeople who really enjoy travelling every week; they love engaging with new customers and they get a thrill from closing new business, particularly when the commission is good;

- **Do they know the business and the industry?** This helps them to hit the ground running. Having said that, good salespeople can sell anything; the process is usually the same across most industries. But it makes a huge difference when a salesperson can lift the phone to someone they already know and offer something that is well-positioned and relevant to the customer; it can significantly reduce sales cycles and happy customers become great references;
- **Communication skills:** Do they speak well? Can they produce good presentations? Are they ever stuck for words on any topic?
- **Check their background:** What do other people say about them? Look at their LinkedIn profile; link to them and check their contacts. Do they know all the people in the industries that you want them to know? Call people you know who may know them and get on-the-record and off-the-record references;
- **Do they present themselves well:** Customers don't like to see sloppy salespeople with slept-in clothes or, even worse, hung-over and stinking of alcohol. I hired a guy who presented really well at interview but, when he arrived for work on the first day, he was in jeans, wearing a gold necklace, gold rings, gold bracelet, tattoos on his arms, chewing gum and he definitely had been out on the town the night before. His sales achievements matched the look and he did not last long – but it cost us time and money to find this out.

Get your sales presentation right

Your value proposition makes clear what you are selling and the benefits to your target customers. Unless as CEO you are clear on this, you cannot expect your salespeople to know it or to make it up as they go along. It is your responsibility to make sure that the business is very clear about its value proposition for your target customers and the products and services it offers.

Your sales team can help you to shape this, but you need to deliver it yourself. The delivery usually takes the form of a well-written sales presentation that a salesperson can rely on in front of customers. To do this well can take weeks and much iteration of the same materials to get it right. Put real effort into this. I would go as far as to say that there is no point in hiring a sales team until you get this done and done well.

A good exercise is to write a two-page brochure for your product or service. This exercise will identify the most important features and benefits for a sales pitch, the pictures that best illustrate the product/service, the call-to-action one-liners and how you make it compelling with commercial references or statistics that you know the target customer will respond to.

Focus on winning strategic customers

It never ceases to amaze me how companies leave their salespeople to work out the target market for themselves, without any involvement from senior management. If they target the wrong market, your salespeople will be busy fools chasing sales that will never close or chasing sales that will never generate any profits.

There may be a strategic reason to win a certain type of customer – to prove the business model, to enter a new market, or to act as a reference for your product or service – even though you know that they will not generate profits for you. But this needs to be planned by identifying the targets, prioritizing them in order of importance to the business and then moving forward to larger customers as you get more references.

When I set up Nautique there was only one customer that I focused on: the cosmetics buyer in Brown Thomas, the most important cosmetics store in Ireland. When she was happy, it was the key to winning all other customers; they fell like skittles once I was able to reference Brown Thomas. To this day, I always try to work with the largest reference customer possible, or one that is strategically important so they act as a reference to help win other customers.

In MyGoodPoints, we targeted KPMG as a Payroll Giving Partner to use our new service because they were potentially the toughest customer to win. KPMG is the largest accountancy practice in the world; they are the most conservative type of professionals in the world (accountants) and as auditors, they scrutinize everything before they accept it as being OK. To win them as a first reference customer was the key to winning other customers because, as a reference, there was no one tougher; if it was good enough for them, then it would be good enough for any other organization in the world. We are now engaged with other global organizations and no one questions the validity of the service, the technology, the processes, etc.

Build a predictable sales pipeline

You need to clearly define your sales process and turn it into a pipeline specific to your business.

You know (or you should know) the key milestones or stages that are required for your business to engage with a new customer to the point of signing a contract and generating revenues. The more clearly you define and refine the key steps to closing a customer, the more predictable your sales pipeline will become and the easier it will be to scale the sales process by adding new salespeople whose performance can be tracked easily through their progress in the sales process.

For example, in the software business, there can be a long sales cycle but typically, after a first meeting, you add the customer to the pipeline if there is a clear interest in the product. The next step might be to get a non-disclosure agreement (NDA) in place; this shows that the customer is willing to make the effort to go forward. The next step might be a workshop with senior stakeholders; then a trial of the product, moving to commercial discussions, draft contracts, etc. If you have 10 different stages, you can express them in percentage terms: 10% to 20% etc. Thus, for a customer to get to 100% (a signed contract with a commitment to pay), they need to go through all of the previous nine stages.

Your pipeline and its predictability are very important when you start to scale the business. Any external third party, such as an investor, will place value on your pipeline if it is shown to be robust and predictable; in fact, it will be a key focus point for VC investors or in an exit process. A predictable pipeline takes time to develop and always involves direct engagement by the CEO and senior management.

Make sure the basic selling skills are being applied

As the CEO of a company that wants to scale it is critical that you make sure that:

- All of the sales team are clear about the sales process; and
- They follow a basic sales engagement model.

I don't propose to teach you how to run your sales process here but some basic questions that need to be answered in any sales engagement include:

- Does the client have a budget to close a deal?
- Is there a significant pain point that they need to address?
- Who owns the revenue line and what are their targets?
- Is this deal important to them in terms of new revenue?
- Is it strategic to them?
- What are their key buying drivers?
- Do we clearly understand their decision-making process?

11: Achieving Your Sales Targets

- Who needs to sign off? When do they sign off? What is needed to sign off?
- Is an RFI (Request for Information) or RFP (Request for Proposal) process required by procurement?
- What are the contract values that move the decision from the person you are dealing with into a formal process with procurement, where they are obliged to get proposals from other companies? How can we avoid this? What are the criteria to avoid other parties being evaluated as part of the process, etc.?
- Do we have a key sponsor in the customer who really believes in our product or service and has a position of authority to represent our interests and to drive this through to a sale?
- What other projects are going on within the customer's organization? How are they prioritized? Can we fall foul of outside issues such as the customer being sold to a third party, etc.?
- What does the competitive offer look like? Is it better, cheaper, etc? How can we win against our competition for this sale?

It's not rocket-science. But it is critical to your success in accelerating the growth of your business.

Make sure all the decision-makers are on board

Following a sales process is important. I consider myself a good salesperson: I try to build relationships with key decision-makers; I go to the top to get decisions made; and I try to push things forward all the time with the classic end-of-meeting question: "So where are we now and what do we need to do next?" But I have made huge mistakes by not following a sales process.

One engagement taught me a lesson: we were selling a software service to Smart in the Philippines, one of the largest mobile operators there, with over 25 million subscribers. Winning this account would make a huge difference to our business. I had a good engagement with the Head of Products; then I met the Head of Marketing and ultimately I met the CEO. After giving him the outline of the service, he shook my hand and said, "We really want to do this. I really like your service. Let's get on with deploying it." I contained my excitement at the meeting but, when I got outside, I immediately got on the phone to our Chairman to share the good news, "We won Smart!" Congratulations were shared as we celebrated our huge success. But a week later, I received a call from our lead in Smart telling me that the deal could not proceed because their own engineering team had been working on a similar project and were already committed to their own in-house solution. I had ignored the basic sales process step of covering off *all* the key decision-makers to make sure that no one could or would block the deal. I have never repeated that mistake.

Learn to say "No"

Sometimes, with sales of innovative products and services, you find that lots of so-called customers are happy to meet with you to find out what is happening in the market, who is doing what and what new services are coming down the line. However, they have no intention of ever buying from you – they just want to learn from you. In the motor trade, they are known as 'tire-kickers.' You learn to spot these types of engagements over time and with experience.

I worked with a company that was selling to a very large European customer. The CEO was very excited about the prospects of winning a huge contract, but after a deep dive into the sales engagement to date it was obvious to me that the customer was simply stealing their ideas to help them build their own solution. They held workshop after workshop, doing demos and showing all of the workings for their product, with no detailed discussions about budgets, commercials, etc. The CEO did not believe me when I warned him to be cautious. Some weeks later, the engagement was terminated by the customer and only a few months later they launched their own remarkably similar version of the service. Needless to say, there was no NDA signed between the parties but, even if there had been, it is almost impossible for a company to challenge a customer like this for copying.

The problem with engagements like this is that they suck up a lot of your scarce resources: cash, people, time, engineering, etc. You simply cannot afford to let this happen when you are scaling your business. Following a simple sales process and being prepared to say "No" as often as you say "Yes" is a good skill to learn. But when you say "No," you must mean "No" – you must be prepared to walk away.

Learn to say "No" to engagements that are impossible to close given your current position in the market, too expensive to service, not likely to be profitable, etc. Saying "No" to customer engagements is difficult but it is one of the skills that a CEO must bring to the table when you are scaling a business.

11: Achieving Your Sales Targets

Saying "No" can produce some incredible results

I was engaged with a very large potential customer where we were being squeezed on price to the point that it was no longer worth the effort. In the end, I simply said "No." The customer was amazed that we were going to walk away – but we did.

Some months later, the customer asked us to come in again to discuss the commercials. Because I had written off the engagement, I put forward what we would ideally like to get in terms of revenue, deciding that we were not going to move from this position – it was a "take it or leave it" offer. A few weeks later, the customer came back to us and said they would take it. We got all the terms we were after in the first place by simply saying "No" – and meaning it.

Talk to your customers and listen

One of the most important things to do in any customer engagement is to listen to the customer. Only by listening can you hear all of the pain points that exist for that customer. And then you can shape your offering to fit their needs.

The best sales engagements don't need any slides. The most engaging conversations with customers are those that flow naturally. You need to listen, listen, listen to the customer. I never start a sales engagement without asking the customer to tell me about their own company, what they do, where they fit and what are the most important issues that they are facing at that time, where are their pain points and what are their top priorities in terms of new revenues, etc. When you listen you can tailor your pitch to meet their needs, focusing on their key drivers – this way you get their attention and get them excited about how you can solve their problems.

I sat in on a sales call with an experienced sales director who was pitching a new service into a very large and sophisticated customer. At the beginning of the call the sales head asked the customer to tell him what were the key areas that the customer was trying to address in their business. The customer launched into one such area while the sales guy said nothing at all, he simply listened. When the customer finished talking the sales guy simply said "Are there any other areas that you are focused on?" and silence. The silence seemed to last a long time until the customer started to talk again. When the customer finished the sales guy asked the same question again. At this stage I thought he was taking this approach too far, but he sat there and said nothing for what seemed to be a very long time and, to my amazement, the customer opened up again and launched in to a third area, giving us absolute nuggets of information that allowed us to push all of their pain points with our pitch.

Nearly every salesperson I have ever worked with – including myself – struggles with long periods of silence. We simply cannot stop talking and pitching to the customers – it's what we do. Try to stop doing this – try to extract the nuggets of information that the customer is willing to give if you simply listen to them and give them the chance to speak before you say anything at all.

When you listen to your potential customer you learn to flex your solutions to meet their needs. This can mean a significant shift in focus from what you are doing today to what they want to buy, or it can be as simple as changing the description of your product or service. I have seen dramatic shifts, where a product is radically altered to address a market opportunity for a specific customer based on their needs and this sends the company down a new path that they did not expect – and it turns out to be the key to their success, allowing them to scale the business based on the new focus.

Having said this, you don't want to jump all over the place based on every individual customer's specific needs and wants. This can damage your business if there is no focus in terms of your products and solutions, so you need to make a strategic decision to pursue a certain direction that you know you can scale with other customers.

When you have customers, talk to them and listen to them all the time. This will help you to shape your products as you go forward and continue to please them and retain them, but also it will help you to scale and win more customers by better understanding the benefits of your solutions for your customers.

Talking to your customers means that you, as CEO, talk to your customers and know your customers well. Because you hear things in a different way to other people in your organization, you will pick up strategic opportunities and key pain points by speaking directly to customers, which others on your team might miss. By listening to your customers on a regular basis, you also will pick up on new opportunities to sell those customers more or to retain them against a competitor who is offering them more.

Thank your customers – personally

CEOs trying to scale their business should say "Thank you" to their customers on a regular basis. It is such a simple thing to do. By calling your customers as the CEO, you will be amazed at the positive feedback you will receive. In many instances, simply because you lifted the phone and said "Hi," they will open up to you and offer you new business or tell you that you have a problem and that the business is at risk of being lost, thus allowing you the opportunity to react and save the business.

Even with all the responsibilities that you have as CEO, you should not be too busy to do this. This is one of the most important tasks that any CEO can perform on behalf of the business. One thing that I have observed in my career is that, the more successful a company is, the more focused their CEO is on their customers – or maybe it's the other way around? The best CEOs are the best salesperson in their organization because they have a passion for their customers, they really understand and serve their needs and they respond to customers as the most important task in the business.

If you don't understand your customers, how will you make sure your products and services meet their needs? You must live out your own beliefs in terms of servicing customers' needs. If you can make this part of the culture of your business, it will have a huge impact on the ability of your business to scale.

Build relationships with your customers

In this new world where markets are truly global and products and services can be sold to customers in any country, it is increasingly important to build relationships with your customers. Knowing who your customers are, what they like and addressing their needs in a targeted and personal way can be the difference between success and failure. Look at how Amazon grew its business as an online retailer, simply by tracking its customers' behavior and making recommendations based on what was relevant to customers and by making it very easy for them to buy with a one-click purchasing process.

Digital Trading is all about providing tools to business owners that allow them to know who their customers are and to build a profile based on what they buy and how often they visit, etc., thus allowing the creation of communications and offers based on this profile so it is targeted and personalized. I firmly believe that every business owner in the world, large and small, some day will have this product or one like it, so they can better manage their relationships with customers in a competitive globalized marketplace.

As you build a relationship with customers you also build their trust. This is important when the customer is looking at buying new products or services from you and other providers. If they trust you based on their experience they are much more likely to buy from you again as opposed to trying out someone new – even if you are not cheaper or better. Often when you are selling innovative products or services, by building a relationship with the customer where they trust you to deliver, they are inclined to buy what you are delivering today, which may not be so different to other suppliers, trusting in the relationship and your ability to deliver the innovation in the future. How often do we hear "I won't get fired for buying IBM"? People trust IBM to deliver –

they also trust that, if things do go wrong, IBM has the resources to correct the problems. So customers trust IBM and continue to buy more from them, even though there may be better products and services available from other companies at lower prices.

Make your sales effort scalable through partners

If your product or service is ahead of the market, giving you a lead on your competitors, unless you accelerate your sales effort you will miss the market opportunity and never be able to scale your business because the market will have passed you by.

Scaling your sales effort can be very expensive, particularly if you have international sales that require people on the ground in different countries selling to your target customers. In many cases, the answer to scaling your sales effort lies not in hiring more sales resources internally but in partnering with other sales channels that can work with you and help you get to market quickly and more cost-effectively.

In imagine it was the agents who really accelerated our growth; the direct sales team were good but we could never scale that approach – it just cost too much to run and too much time and resources to manage. By appointing agents who were paid commissions on sales only, we had a very predictable business model. If we wanted more customers, we simply got more agents and/or paid them more money to increase their sales effort – it was very effective.

Retail presence is another important route to market if you are selling items that are fast-moving consumer goods (FMCG). In Meteor one of our most effective sales channels was Xtravision. Its sheer number of stores made our numbers work; if each store sold a cell phone per day, the numbers added up very quickly. Making products available to the mass market is important if you want to scale your business – for example, if you sell a food item and you get it stocked in Tesco across all its stores, you will go from zero volume to thousands of items per day almost overnight. People will buy your products if they are available, well-displayed and of reasonable quality and price.

Going to market with partners has its merits but it also has its difficulties. I have seen many companies put a huge amount of effort into getting a deal done with a major partner, flying all over the world, paying huge legal fees and sometimes even changing products and services to fit the relationship – all for the pot of gold at the end of the rainbow that never came. Major companies often take on board new partners to get insight into innovative products and services; in some cases, they do discuss these new products or services with customers but usually the difficulty is that your product/service does not register on their scale of revenue targets and there is no specific incentive for the salespeople to sell it, so it sits in a large portfolio of products and services that never get sold.

You need to know exactly how to use a larger partner to help you accelerate your business growth. Accept that, in most cases, you will need to do all of the work on the ground with customers, including the sales process, trials and live demonstrations if you get that far – in effect, you get to use your partner's contact database and their customer relationships but little else. You also must find a way to motivate your partner's salespeople to sell your product/service. In many cases your revenue will never be enough to help them get anything out of a sale of your product/service, so you need to build a relationship with the sales team. You may find that your product/service is sufficiently innovative for the team to use as a door-opener or to show how innovative their company is; this might help the salesperson to engage his customers around other products and services from which he can make his commission.

Be careful not to build up partnerships that look great on paper but deliver no revenues. You are better to focus on smaller players who are hungrier for your business, who are on the ground and where your service can impact their top and bottom line. Put yourself into the shoes of the salesperson and make sure that he/she is motivated to sell; this may mean offering a commission or incentive structure in partnership with the channel partner that drives the salespeople. Don't be shy about networking directly with your partner's salespeople and pushing them as hard as you can to work for you or even to give you introductions so you can take the ball yourself and run with it. You might need to do all the work and then sign a commission check to your partner at the end of the day for doing little or nothing, but it is still worth it to get high-level introductions. Do it often enough and you might become important to them and they will get engaged.

I remember experiencing this first-hand with BT after I sold my business to them. My chairman at the time was an old BT guy who knew how the company worked; he compared it to a sitting elephant – you need to push and pull to get it to stand up but, when it starts to move, there is no stopping it and the rewards can be great. I certainly pushed and pulled the elephant for many months and eventually they started to engage and delivered us our first customers.

Be careful what you wish for

If you are successful in getting a partner on board and they are selling your service effectively, you need to consider how you are going to support this effort.

At one stage with BT they generated so many potential engagements with customers all over the world that we did not know which way to turn. We flew here, there and everywhere at their request, but soon realized that we could not close sales with this approach. Selling to mobile operators needs focused effort: if the engagement is good and they are likely to buy, you need to be there week after week to support the engagement; this is not possible if you are a small company trying to scale your business.

Having the right people in your own organization to support channel sales is very important: key account managers as opposed to hard-nosed salespeople; technical support/pre-salespeople who can visit customers with your partner; reporting systems that allow you to pay your partner or get paid by them, etc. When I first engaged with BT I did not know what a pre-sales engineer was, let alone have any of them on the team; I soon learned and hired them, but all of this costs money and time and it could be a long time before you see the payback for this investment.

How to capture your sales in your Accelerated Growth Plan slide deck ...

To capture your sales strategy in one slide, start by describing your sales model: do you go direct to customers or use channel partners or both? Try to illustrate the sales process you use and how predictable it is. Show that your sales effort is focused, well-thought-out and linked to the market opportunity as described earlier.

It might be worth showing a sales pipeline with named customers and the stages that they are at in order to instill confidence in the sales capabilities of your organization. To show this pipeline and the value of the customers in it will require a fully operational sale process so it can act as a driver.

12
HOW DO YOU MAKE MONEY?

- Your business model determines the value of your business
- Beware the 'valley of death'
- Use a minimum monthly commitment fee to cover your basic costs
- Freemium works – but needs deep pockets
- Use your business model to reduce your risk
- A better business model for services
- Be clear about how you make money

Your business model is important because ...

Every business has its business model. To scale your business, you need to get this right; it can be the difference between being able to sell your products or services and not being able to sell them at all.

Business models change as the market changes. For example, software used to be sold for an upfront fee; now customers pay up for it on a pay-as-you-use or software as a service (SaaS). My own business goes to market under this model as it is probably the only way we could sell our service, since there are no capex budgets available in the businesses we sell to today.

Another shift in the market – and change in business model – is offering your services on a revenue share basis. This was unthinkable when ownership of the customers was all-important; today, cash-strapped companies (which include governments and large corporations) are willing to do revenue share deals because this allows them to innovate and potentially grow their revenues without incurring large upfront capital investments that may or may not pay off.

In a recession, new business models (like revenue share) can create huge market opportunities for companies that have the vision and the resources to enter into deals that, in better market conditions, larger customers would not consider. If you can do these deals in a recession, as the market improves you improve with it and potentially make a significant amount of money for a relatively low risk and low investment.

Your business model determines the value of your business

Your chosen business model has a huge impact on the value of your business and your ability to bring in investors or to exit the business.

Take for example the Nespresso coffee machines from Nestlé, one of the most successful and profitable business models in the food industry. To all intents and purposes, Nestlé simply copied the inkjet/laser printer business model where it sells the machine at cost and then generates all the ongoing revenues and substantial profits from selling the capsules that are needed to use the machine. This is a fantastic business model if you can get it right – and Nestlé did. Its marketing and products are so good that it can demand (and get) a huge margin on a capsule that makes a single cup of coffee. If you can find a business model like this and make it work, you have hit on a gold mine.

Beware the 'valley of death'

The difficulty with shifting business models from, say, upfront payments to a revenue share is that it can kill your cashflow. Instead of getting, say, €1 million in the bank on day one, you have to wait three years to earn, say, €2 million – so your cashflow takes a beating, even though the overall value of the contract and its profitability might have increased. This transition in business models is often called the 'valley of death', as so many companies go bust as they migrate from one model to another due to cashflow issues.

To survive, you need strong cash reserves or an understanding investor. But when you come through to the other side, the good news is that your business is worth a lot more money to potential investors because your revenues are now more predictable and the opportunity for growth is much stronger because you are now linked to the potential success of your customers. You also have an ongoing relationship or partnership with these customers as opposed to a once-off sale where you may never sell anything to that customer again.

But, again, the market is changing: customers are beginning to impose caps on the potential revenue share that suppliers can earn. If this happens to you, you may have little choice but to accept it – however, make sure that the cap is high enough that you can get a good return on your investment over the life of the contract.

Use a minimum monthly commitment fee to cover your basic costs

To help manage your cashflow, you need to be a bit creative with your commercial engagements to make sure that you are covering your costs and making some money from the outset of every engagement.

In my own business, I offer a revenue share model but I also charge upfront payments to run trials for customers, set-up fees to brand and integrate the service for the specific customer, day-rate fees for any bespoke work required to the core platform and then, most important of all, a minimum monthly commitment fee (MMC). This MMC is usually based on your cost of running the service, so hosting, support, third party software licenses, etc. all need to be covered by this fee and it is charged every month for the period of the contract, regardless of any revenues being generated by the service supplied. When revenues are generated, under the MMC model you only receive the portion of the revenue share that exceeds the minimum commitment fee. Essentially, each month you earn the higher of your revenue share or your MMC.

Freemium works – but needs deep pockets

The freemium model is where you offer a free service to mass-market consumers online but, after a period of time, you introduce premium services that the customer must pay for. If you get this right, and the customer enjoys your free service and believes they can derive even better value from your premium service, then they will willingly pay you for the premium component. Companies that have used this business model to great effect include Skype, LinkedIn and Dropbox.

However, you need deep pockets or very low cost operations to pull this off because your success drives the need for more resources to support more (non-paying) customers. The stakes are very high; you need to be sure that you have a runaway success that will be purchased by someone who can leverage the value of these customers or that you can charge enough revenues to the small group of paying customers in the long-term to make profits.

I met an investor from New York who only invests in companies that offer this type of freemium business model but, when he invests, he puts in a significant amount of money and rolls the dice knowing the scale of the potential risk. We have all heard of the successes but, believe me, there are thousands of failures. In fact, the failures are far too high relative to the successes. I did consider this model for Digital Trading but quickly dismissed it, given the level of funding and resources that would be required to pull it off, not to mention the increased risk profile for the business and for me personally.

Use your business model to reduce your risk

Getting a lead in the market with a new business model can give you a significant commercial advantage and can allow you to scale your business fast.

You also can use your business model to remove or reduce your risk in scaling your business. I recently used a website to buy new tires for my car. They were great value when compared to the prices in the local garage but, for this business model to work, the company needed to offer the customer the ability to get the tires fitted. So it has a network of approved partners that will fit the type for an extra charge of €10 per tire; the tires are delivered to the local fitter that you choose. It's a brilliant business model – everyone wins. In particular, the business is able to scale because the commercial model works.

A better business model for services

Usually when pricing a service to your customer, you arrive at your price by taking your costs and adding a fair profit.

A better way is to come at the problem from the other end: start by valuing the commercial benefit of the service for the customer and then take a fair portion of this regardless of your costs. The benefits to your customers can be measured in increasing revenues, increasing the whole life value of their customers, reducing the costs of operating their business, etc. Customers usually are willing to take this model because the benefits are very clear if the ROI is solid. This can create a hugely profitable business, if the problem you solve for your customers is both big enough and quantifiable.

Be clear about how you make money

When you are explaining your business model to investors or other external third parties, it is important that you are clear about how you make money and where revenue growth opportunities will come from.

Many businesses that sell products also sell consulting services to support their cashflow while their products build traction in the market. However, it is often difficult to reduce the dependency on consulting revenues as the business grows, but investors put little or no value on revenues that are generated through consulting.

So it is important to classify your revenues correctly: annuity-based revenues are more valuable than once-off fees so shifting business models can add value to your business. Where you have a mix of revenue types, distinguish between them and clearly identify how your business model works for potential investors. And you must show the reduced dependency over time on professional services fees as your product revenues through annuity-type contracts grow.

How to capture your business model in your Accelerated Growth Plan slide deck ...

It's important that you and your team clearly understand your business model and how much money you make as you grow. It is also important to show your audience how you make money and how much money you can make if the business grows. Illustrate how your business model works by walking through a typical customer following the money flow.

By the time you finish this slide, your audience should have a very clear understanding of how your revenues are generated, how profitable you are today and how this profitability will grow as the business grows. The simpler your commercial model, the easier it is to implement and sell to others.

When you are explaining your commercial model to external third parties, it is important that you are clear about how you make money and where the revenue growth opportunities will come from.

So, for example, many businesses that sell products also sell consulting services to support their cashflow while their products get traction in the market. It is often difficult to reduce the dependency on the consulting revenues as the business grows, but investors put little or no value on revenues that are generated through consulting. They separate these revenues out and then offer a lesser value for the product revenues.

So it is important to classify your revenues correctly. Annuity-based revenues are more valuable than once-off fees, so shifting to this model can add more value to your business.

Where there is a mix of revenue types, you need to distinguish between them and to identify clearly how your commercial model works for potential investors.

13

HOW DO YOU BEAT THE COMPETITION?

- To beat the competition, understand marketing
- Know your competitors well
- Be able to defend your competitive advantage
- If you lose business to a competitor, find out why
- Friend or foe?
- Always assume that the competition will copy you
- Don't fear the competition

Understanding your competitors is important because ...

You can never underestimate the power of your competitors. Competitors are a fact of life and, in business, if you find a gap in the market that you get to explore and generate huge profits from, it won't be long before competitors get to hear about it and descend *en masse* on the opportunity that you have discovered. In a truly competitive marketplace, you don't get to dominate and take super-normal profits from it for the long term. Although in some markets, monopolies exist under government protection, for the purposes of this book I assume that you operate in an open and competitive marketplace.

To beat the competition, understand marketing

Although I studied commerce in college and marketing was one of my subjects, my first lessons in marketing did not happen in the classroom but on the street as a street-trader. While at college, in the summer I bought and sold strawberries, buying locally where there was an oversupply and selling further away where there was scarcity and getting a good margin in the process. My average load was 1,000 punnets of strawberries, which I bought for 75p each and sold for £1.50; the trick was to sell everything I had in one trip, as anything left over at the end of the day was wastage and ate into my profits.

One day when I arrived in a town, my usual spot in the middle of the town square was already taken by a local farmer who was sitting in the opening to a small dog trailer, with two or three punnets of strawberries beside him and a small hand-written sign saying "Fresh Strawberries. Picked Today. Only IR£1". My two helpers panicked as they were on commission, and we had strawberries that had been picked the night before, had sat in a van with no cooling system overnight and then travelled across the country for several hours – worse, our selling price was IR£1.50 per punnet. Since it was too late to switch to another town, as far as they were concerned we were stuffed.

But we took every single strawberry out of the van, lined the punnets up in large trays covering a huge area of the town square with red strawberries. I told my helpers, "If anyone asks for the price or wants to buy, just say we will be back to them after we set up." A small crowd started to gather. When we had all of the strawberries on display, you could not help noticing the sea of red from any point in the town. The crowd got bigger. Then I told my helpers, "Start selling very slowly, tell people our price is IR£1.50 but fuss with change and bags and take as long as possible to sell." As we did this, people started to get anxious: as people saw other people buying and getting impatient, others wanted to buy until we nearly had a frenzy on our hands. Then I instructed my two helpers to sell, sell, sell as fast as they could. We were sold out in less than two hours and I mean sold out, not one punnet left. In the meantime, throughout all of this buying frenzy, the farmer beside us had not sold anything even though his product was superior to ours and his price was substantially less.

This taught me my first – and arguably, most important – lesson in how to deal with competition: you don't need to have the best products or the best prices to beat the competition, as long as you get marketing.

Know your competitors well

Don't they say "keep your friends close and your enemies closer"? It is important to know who your competitors are and how they can win against you in the marketplace. CEOs who say that their company doesn't have any competition or who know nothing about their competition are naive to say the least and rarely get to accelerate their growth because they underestimate their competitors. It is very important to study and understand your competitors.

In imagine, we were winning so many corporate customers that one of our competitors started to follow our sales teams in cars to see who they were selling to and then tried to protect or win back the customers.

Competition can get very dirty and some companies know no boundaries when it comes to protecting their own turf. I know companies that have sent their employees to work for a competitor to gain knowledge of their strategies, customers, products, etc. and then used that knowledge when the employee returned to the mothership. Many companies buy their competitors' products as soon as they hit the market, just to take them apart and copy them.

Competition also can be intense and bloody. I have been beaten up (metaphorically, of course) by some giants in my time. Twice, I have had to back down from pursuing what my legal advisors told me were open-and-shut cases, where the law was clearly on my side, simply because I could not afford the cost – legal fees plus the distraction from growing my business – to fight on. I just had to fold my hand and walk away from the table. It rankled then – and does still. But I understand the consequences of taking on giant competitors.

Knowing your competitors means that you know who they are, what markets they operate in, the price of their products, their products themselves and everything associated with them. In other words, you need to know your key competitors' value proposition as well as you know your own.

Be able to defend your competitive advantage

Once you know your competitors well, you need to be able to defend your competitive advantage in front of your target customers, investors or any other stakeholders in your business. In particular, it is important to be able to show your customers how you are better than the competition – the proof lies in the customer choosing you as a supplier and not the competition. Some companies use a table of features, where all the features that they have highlighted are ticked for their product or service and their competitors are shown to be lacking in different areas. But this can be dangerous, as your competitor can create its own table and define its competitive advantage against you.

It is better to focus on the customer benefits rather than product features, since incumbent competitors are often slower to react to improved benefits because their products are complex, too expensive, too slow to deploy, too expensive to maintain, etc. If you are up against a giant, they will be slow to react but you can be sure that, if you eat too much of their lunch, eventually they will react and make a move to defend their market. When they do, be prepared to move forward again through innovation or a change of commercial model or speed to market or cost savings that they cannot match – and keep on moving ahead.

If you lose business to a competitor, find out why

When you compete for business and lose the contract, make sure that you find out why you lost. This is critical and valuable information to your business as you plan to scale. It is amazing how many companies simply chalk up the loss and move on. But, if you know why you lost, you can do something about it the next time you come up against the same competitor.

Larger customers are used to providing feedback to potential suppliers on why they won or lost; it's part of their buying process. Smaller customers are not used to this, so use your position as CEO to make clear how important the loss is to your company – lift the phone and ask why you lost. And make sure that part of your sales process is to make sure that every lost deal is tracked until you find out why.

Friend or foe?

Competitors or potential competitors can be your friend or your foe, depending on how you approach them in the market. It is OK to nip away at the fringes of a competitor's core market but, when you start to take too many of their customers, you will get a reaction.

Instead you can choose to partner with them to deliver your more innovative product or new business model or whatever your competitive advantage is, if it helps them to win more market share against other competitors.

Or you can choose to antagonize them so much that they simply buy your company and take you out of the market.

Or you could upset them so much that they choose to kill you by bringing down prices to a level that you cannot match just to take you out of the market; if they are very big and you are small they can afford to do this.

Smaller competitors often underestimate the lengths to which a larger competitor will go to put them out of business. Some larger organizations have a strategy to stop emerging competitors when they are small to prevent them even getting a foothold in their market; it's easier and cheaper to kill off emerging competitors when they are small.

Always assume that the competition will copy you

It's said that to be copied is a compliment or flattery. I have had many different products or service or strategies copied by competitors. Sometimes, I am amazed at how fast the ideas can be copied; it shows that the competitor is tracking what you are doing and preparing to copy all the time to cloud your competitive advantage. Larger companies are very good at using PR and other forms of marketing messages to confuse customers into believing that they offer the same or better service than you do. Often when you are selling innovation against a larger and incumbent supplier, they are happy to tell the customer, "If you ask us for that, we can deliver it". Then, if they win the business, they go to build the product or service, which may take a lot of time but they string out the customer until it's ready.

Try to make sure that you don't help your competitors to copy your products or services. This happens all the time. For example, a user manual for your product can become a blueprint for your competitors to copy once they get their hands on it – and inevitably, they do. I have manuals for all the competitor products that I admire or fear. Requests for a Proposal (RFPs) that larger companies put out to get competitive bids from different companies are full of valuable information and typically are drafted with the help of the chosen partner. If you are this supplier, then you may be able to persuade your customer to include your competitive advantages (USPs) as part of the proposal criteria – this may help you win the bid, but it also shows your competitors exactly what the customer wants to buy, giving them enough information to go and build it.

Don't fear the competition

If you fear your competition you should never start a business in the first place. Whatever industry or market or territory you choose there always will be competition. But there is also always room for a new player in any industry as long as you do it faster, better, cheaper, etc.

I have always taken on big industries. Yes, in the early days, I was beaten by the competition eventually but, as I get older and wiser, I think I am able to stay ahead of the competition and ultimately win.

But what does winning mean? It could mean partnering with the competition; or selling out to them; or accepting a smaller market niche, etc. There are many different tactics you can use to beat your competition, including:

- **Innovation:** As a new entrant to a market, typically you will be more innovative; continuing to lead the market with innovation can help you to beat the competition;
- **Marketing:** As discussed earlier, you can outsell your competitors who may have better products if you are better at marketing;
- **Understanding customers:** If you understand the customer benefits of your product or service better than your competitors, you can win out; for example, if your customers value quick delivery, then even though your competitors supply a better product, the fact that it takes months to implement while you can deliver in days, will bring you business;
- **New business models:** Defining a new business model can help you to beat the competition; for example, if the customer does not have the budget to buy the big software platform that your competitor is selling and the competitor is not geared up to allow for a revenue share model, then you might be able to win simply because your business model meets the customer's need to avoid an upfront cost;
- **Better operations and cost control:** Ryanair showed how to beat the competition in the airline business by offering cheaper fares that the competitors simply could not match due to the way they run their businesses.

How to capture your competition in your Accelerated Growth Plan ...

When you are preparing your slide for competition, the objective is to show that you know who your competition are and how they are better or worse than you and in what areas.

Many companies list the functionality of their product and then show green dots against their own functionality, while placing red dots against the competition. But this does not show that you really understand your competition: you need to know whether they have more capital or better routes to market, what could happen if they decided to stop you in the market, how they price, how they compare to you in the customers' minds, etc. You need to show in one slide that you really understand your competitors and their strengths and weaknesses compared to yours. I often use a grid and place the competitors against my company based on a number of key factors – say four at most, like technology, scale, customers and capital. Use words and pictures but discuss some key areas to show you really understand your competition.

14

YOU NEED A GREAT TEAM

- Good people in business are good people full-stop
- Trust above all
- As CEO, you must be involved in recruiting
- Understand the person before recruiting them
- Check more than just references
- Get the right people in the right roles
- Know when it's time to step aside as CEO
- Scaling people requires systems
- Take a chance on people
- Communications is part of your job as CEO
- Make meetings useful

Your team is important because ...

Without good people in your business, you cannot scale unless you are Superman (or Superwoman) and can do everything yourself. You'll soon find out that you are not – and cannot. I have been privileged to work with some great people in my career, but having great people around you generally is not an accident – like everything else, you need to work hard at it: selecting, recruiting, managing and exiting people as and when the business requires it.

I was driving in my car one day with one of my children. He said to me that he did not like a particular person who works for me because that person is very quiet and does not seem to be much fun. I explained that this person was a genius and, without him, I could not run my company. I also explained that people are all different; we have different talents and only by bringing together a range of different talents can we build a successful company – hopefully enjoying ourselves in the process.

This is a hard concept for many business leaders to follow. We tend to hire people who are like ourselves; the more they are like us, the more we want to hire them. I saw an extreme example of this in a medium-sized company with approximately 50 people: they were all engineers and they were all the same; each had a different role but the engineer heading up sales was not an outgoing extrovert who told the odd white lie to close the sale – he was quiet, introvert and very factual, a classic engineer. We must learn to work with people who are not the same as us; getting the mix of skills and personalities right can be very effective.

I also found that getting people right from the outset saves a lot of heartache – even one bad apple in an organization can spread discontent. Some people are a 'glass half-empty;' in fact, some people can see only the empty glass – they can be so negative that they bring other people down with them and nothing is possible, everything is a problem. Don't just hire optimistic people – you need the balance of realistic people too – but if you have an overly negative person on your team, get rid of them. It is like having tin cans tied to the back of your car; they will just keep rattling away until they are cut off.

I usually ask the existing team to be involved in the recruitment process, since they will need to get on with the person being recruited.

Good people in business are good people full-stop

I think that having good people in your business means having good people full-stop. This means people who respect their fellow-workers, who are kind, who have good family values, who have some humility and who like working in a team – all these things are common to good people, so this should be the first criterion for recruiting. Specific skills and experience come second and you can assume these in the person you recruit because if they don't have the basic skills for the job then you should not be interviewing them in the first place.

If someone turns out to be a bad person – they are disrespectful to others, bullying or go as far as fighting (which I have seen in my career) – then I simply get rid of them. I don't tolerate this behavior, no matter how good the person is at their job. You need a motivated team to scale a business, so no one person is important enough to be excused for such behavior.

I don't have a problem with people who express difficulties with their work/life balance, who try to balance work with home. I respect those who see the importance of home life. I know for a fact that people who are content in life tend to be content in work and they can bring a lot to the workplace, so getting this right is a very important part of getting work right and I do all I can to accommodate people who respect the balance and flexibility that a company can offer them. But they need to respect the business and get the balance right for the business too.

Trust above all

For me, the most important characteristic that I look for in building a team is trust. After that comes life values and only then do I look at their skillset and experience. Needless to say, if a person is weak on skills and experience, they don't get to the table in the first place, but when choosing between equally qualified people I always choose the person that shows these qualities. As we move to a more mobile workforce where people can work from home or on the move, knowing that you can trust them to get the job done and to respect the company's resources and use them to best effect for the benefit of the business is a huge part of how we need to work going forward.

I operate a virtual company where everyone works remotely. I bring them together for strategy meetings or to agree on a plan of action. This means that I need to trust everyone to do their job, to put in the hours they are being paid for, to charge expenses only for what is fair and reasonable and to do their job diligently and effectively without supervision. I believe this is the model of the future and it is a critical component to accelerating the growth of your business. You can hire people from anywhere in the world with the technology we have today; you can manage them and get good quality work from them no matter where they are but the criteria for recruiting them needs to be the same.

As CEO, you must be involved in recruiting

One of the most difficult things in business and in scaling a business is hiring good people. If you are scaling, you are usually so busy that you struggle to find time to interview and to pay attention to hiring people. You need to get the existing team to do a lot of the initial work in screening candidates but I do not hire anyone without meeting them myself.

When I meet someone at a recruitment interview, I always try to get them on to a life conversation – family, sports, lifestyle, etc. I know that a lot of these areas are off-limits regulations-wise but for me it is the most insightful way to get some view on how good or bad these people will be in your company. I look for flexibility, commonsense, team-playing, ambition, courage (like travelling the world on their own), and discipline (like working hard for a sport or holding down part-time jobs while in college), etc.

I look for people who stand out from the crowd, who are willing to speak their mind but in a respectful way, who are willing to challenge but in a constructive way, who are willing to fight for what is right while keeping a balance. When looking at lots of CVs, I go for 'different:' since the basic skills and qualifications are probably common to all the candidates, what's different about this person? Most importantly, I ask whether they would add a good dynamic to the existing team.

Understand the person before recruiting them

If I am recruiting a senior executive, I always will take them out of the work environment to get a better insight into what they are like as a person. Hosting a dinner in the evening can be a good way to do this: if they drink, I often offer them more to see how they respond; I look at their table manners; I ask myself whether they are good company, how would our customers respond to this person, would I look forward to having dinner with this person if I was travelling to a customer or would the customer enjoy it. Senior executives often rehearse their responses in preparation for an interview, so you need to get past this, which can be difficult to do in a formal interview. Many people get hired on the basis of a good interview but then turn out to be a totally different person than the one you thought you were hiring.

This type of informal interview has always served me very well and, from extensive experience, I tend to be right when I make my final decision.

Check more than just references

When it comes to getting references from potential new employees, I always assume that the references were written by their best friend, so typically they are hugely exaggerated. And, since in this new world of litigation, employers are afraid to give someone a bad reference, references from previous employers tend to be bland or generic, saying nothing of any importance. So I always go around the system and follow up with people I know or someone I know who would know the candidate or a former work colleague.

You will get a true reference only if you are off-the-record and on the phone; no one will write anything bad about another person even if they were awful at their job. Even if you don't know the person you need to talk to, if you can build their trust on a phone call they usually open up and give some real insights into the person you are hiring. And what they don't say can be as revealing as anything they do say.

Hiring people you know, or where you know their family or friends, is a good way to make sure that you don't get recruitment badly wrong – as they say, the devil you know is better than the one you don't.

Get the right people in the right roles

Sometimes, to scale a business, you need to fire people and to replace them with better people who can do a better job. Like everyone, I hate firing people. Unfortunately I have had to fire a lot of people in my career, some due to downsizing the business and others due to lack of performance or lack of fit with the business. It is never easy but I have learned how to do this effectively: the most important tip is to make sure that it is never a surprise to the employee; if they are surprised by the conversation, then you have a bigger problem on your hands and the process can be much more difficult. This means plenty of reviews with staff, giving them feedback, asking for specific improvements, giving more feedback and then getting to the point where they finally admit that it is not working for them. They need to understand why they are being asked to leave and accept it as the only way that you and they both can move forward.

As an organization grows, it can be difficult to grow the team in line with the business needs. Often a business is started by a bunch of friends or colleagues that worked together before; this is great at the start-up stage but can cause problems as the business grows. Because they were first in, the original team tends to take the lead roles, like head of engineering or head of sales; as new people join, these heads tend to rise. But their skills may not be suited to the bigger role or they may not have the breadth of experience that allows them to do a good job for a larger business. Since this then makes for a difficult conversation with one of your friends who helped you start the business, many founder CEOs don't go there until it is too late.

Know when it's time to step aside as CEO

A VC once asked me how I knew that it was the right time for me to leave my own business or step aside as the CEO. For me, this is simple: I love the chase and the excitement of starting a new venture; I love working with all the people and customers that come on the journey; but when we get to the end of the road and the business has perfected the product or service for a defined group of customers and just needs to continue to do the same thing day in and day out to grow, then I get bored and I start to look at new projects, either within the business or externally. Several times I have stepped aside and taken the role of board member and head of strategy in my own company where I get to continue to innovate and have fun.

Scaling people requires systems

When you start to scale, you need to put in place formal systems for reporting, for providing feedback to staff, for communicating and for making decisions and implementing projects within the business. If you do not do this, the business will fall into chaos very quickly. This is a big challenge for many founder CEOs who have never worked in a large corporation before. Even if you have corporate experience it is still difficult as you change the rules of engagement that made the business an exciting place to work for the existing team.

Often you need to accept that a scaling business needs a different senior team to bring it to the next level, particularly if the current team does not have the skills. Even if they do have the skills, they might find that they just don't like it any more: "things aren't the way they used to be". I often hear this statement from employees who were part of the start-up team. Usually, you can't solve these problems – the people will never be happy again in the larger organization. If this is the case they are better off leaving; and you are better off encouraging them to leave (assuming they no longer play a critical role in the organization) as the company cannot carry unhappy employees who ultimately become demotivated and whose unhappiness can spill over to other staff.

But some early employees make the transition and grow themselves as the business grows, meeting all the challenges as they come and continuing to do a great job for the business. If they have no experience in a larger organization and you are scaling, give them the support they need to train or to meet other people who can guide them, etc.

As you scale the business you need to be very clear on people's roles. Probably for the first time you will need to write role descriptions for each person in the business. Having learnt the hard way I am a great believer in making sure that everyone knows what their role is in the business and that when a task is assigned, it belongs to one person who must deliver – they may need to go to others to request the support to complete the task but it is clear who owns the task based on their role.

Take a chance on people

But I also believe in finding great talent in the business by allowing people to change their roles. Even if they have no experience in a particular role, if they have the passion and drive to try a new role and if you believe they can do it, then let them try, I have done this often and, when it works, you get highly motivated people who want to prove themselves – when they do, they enjoy it and are grateful for the opportunity they were given. It also drives a culture that anything is possible if you have the drive and determination to succeed.

I also have taken people out of their roles and put them into a more challenging role that often they think they cannot do. I remember asking a relatively low level manager in my business to take my place as a speaker at a conference. The guy was scared and did not want to do it; he worried that he was not good enough, that he did not know enough about the market, that he was not a good speaker, etc., but I knew this guy had leadership qualities way beyond his own belief, so I pushed him into doing it. He did a brilliant job and this gave him the confidence to do more and to grow more in the business – today this guy is a leader as I knew he always would be. Pushing people to do more than they believe they are capable of themselves can give your business amazing results. Many people doubt their ability; try to give them a chance to impress and see how they perform; when they do, they just keep performing over and over again.

Communications is part of your job as CEO

Communications in a company is a critical component of motivating the team and of keeping everyone aligned. As you scale a business it become much more difficult to keep everyone informed about what is happening in the business so people can lose their way. I am a firm believer that everyone who works for a business is a salesperson for the business – that said, they need to know what the business is selling, who it is selling to and the value proposition, how it sells, the pricing, the support, etc. This is up to you as the CEO to get right.

As you scale, the chats at the coffee machine, the informal chats in the pub, the stand-up announcements, etc all disappear. You need to make communications a part of your everyday job, making time for team briefings, sending staff emails to update everyone, selling your brand and your value proposition to everyone in the organization so they get the bigger picture and they know the role they play in delivering the overall business goals and objectives. Often a good vision statement can help – saying "We want to be the best at x" – being the best means everyone is customer-focused and the service you offer is always great at every touchpoint in the business; if not, you fix it.

You also need formal communications systems where people know their roles, and they get regular appraisals and feedback from their managers or colleagues on how they are doing. Employees need to know that there is a career path for them in the organization as they perform and as the business grows. Founder CEOs often hate this part of a growing business, so get help. You don't need to hire a full-time HR manager to make this happen; you can take in a part-time service until you can justify the cost of an in-house resource.

Make meetings useful

As your business scales, you need more formal meetings; in particular, you need to keep your management team aligned with the company objectives and focused on what is important.

I run weekly management meetings or, at the very minimum, monthly meetings where all senior managers are required to attend in person or over the phone. But I always have a specific agenda; I make sure that all stakeholders are asked to give their opinion and then we make a collective decision; I make sure that someone owns the deliverable that we have agreed and that we make a note of this; and at the next meeting I ask for an update on progress. I keep these meetings short – no more than one hour – but then I have specific meetings about specific problems or issues where necessary with the people involved.

I am also a great believer in bringing people together immediately where there is an issue that needs to be resolved. Today with Skype this is easy to do, but any conference facility will help you to get all the stakeholders on a call so you can agree on a way forward. People get used to this behavior and they respond accordingly so things get done quickly and the organization can grow while being agile or flexible as new issues arise; it creates an action-orientated culture or can-do attitude throughout the whole organization. It is also important to bring in everyone that matters on a call like this, senior and junior, so they know that you know what is happening and that decisions are made and projects get implemented.

14: You Need a Great Team

How to capture your team in your Accelerated Growth Plan slide deck ...

Your team is important. Without a good team it is very difficult to scale the business.

Show your organizational structure and, within it, the key people in place today and those that are still missing. Then discuss how the business can manage as it grows and how the new team will emerge if it is not already there. Getting the right organizational structure and the right people in the right roles is critical to scaling a business successfully. This slide should show all of that.

15

FUNDING ACCELERATED GROWTH

- Be creative with your finances
- Cover your costs from the beginning
- Scale on a variable cost/project basis
- Avoid family and friends for funding
- Avoid selling professional services (or at least plan an exit)

Your funding for accelerated growth is important because ...

Like all of the chapters in this section of the book, finance is a key growth component that needs to be understood and controlled if a business wants to scale.

If you have come through the start-up stage and have managed your cash to this point, then you will have a good understanding of what is required to keep the cash flowing. But how do you start to scale if you are short of cash, as most businesses are when they reach the point of wanting to scale?

Managing cash is critical to success. Every business plan can be nearly 100% accurate when it comes to the cash it spends but its revenues are less predictable and inevitably they are slower to materialize. Committing to a big monthly cashburn without guaranteed revenues to meet this cost is basically risking the business. Gone are the days when VCs threw cash at a business so it could take its time to grow and have all the resources needed to make this happen.

Be creative with your finances

Necessity is the great inventor of how to do things better. When you have little or no cash, as many businesses find themselves today, you get creative.

A new commercial model can give you a significant advantage in the market and can allow you to scale your business fast. If you are in a business that has some hardware costs that need to be paid to get access to your product, try to get these costs funded by a finance agreement taken out by your customers so they take the credit risk, or use bank funding in your own business to help manage the cashflow – this can be a bankable business if you have the right type of customers and predictable income streams.

In my experience it is important also to understand the dynamics of your business, the market it operates in and the opportunity it presents in terms of raising finance. Appetite and ability to invest are very subjective issues when dealing with banks and VCs. Some will get your vision or your business opportunity – but many won't. This is the 'leading edge/bleeding edge' dilemma where many investors (and, in particular, banks) simply do not want to invest in anything that is too innovative that they don't understand and that there is no established market for, yet they also want to you to be the only supplier of your service in the market with no competitors!

The biggest issue with raising money is your time. When you start to scale, you are busier than ever and it's not a good time to raise capital. But it needs to be part of your daily tasks, as important as getting that new customer up and running. I remember meeting the founders of Skype some years ago in London: they talked about how in the early days no one could understand the business

15: Funding Accelerated Growth

model – cool technology but no revenues, so no one would invest – they knocked on many doors and all but one closed in their face. But they only needed one!

Good corporate finance is a strategic asset of the business: getting good VCs and investors involved in your business with the right frame of mind and a good working relationship can be like adding rocket fuel. Also managing finances to align with business growth is critically important if you want to accelerate the growth of your business – for example, knowing when to bring in debt equity, when to move to a public offering, when to go for private equity, etc.

US companies are much better at this than European companies: they raise significant finance early to allow them to grow fast. If growth can happen faster through acquisitions, they pursue this as part of their overall business plan and manage it as a core part of their business strategy.

Cover your costs from the beginning

You need to be a bit creative with your commercial arrangements to make sure that you are covering your costs and making some money from the outset of every engagement. In my own business we offer a revenue share commercial model, but I also include up-front payments to run trials for the customers, set-up fees to brand and to integrate the service for the specific customer, day-rate fees for any bespoke work that is required to the core platform and then, most important of all, a minimum monthly commitment fee (MMC). This fee is usually based on the cost of running the service, so it covers hosting, support, third party software licenses, etc. and is charged every month for the period of the contract, regardless of any revenues being generated by the service supplied. It ensures that EVERY engagement covers its costs EVERY month.

I have seen many different types of commercial models that have been designed to allow the company to scale using customer's cash. One company I know sells a software package as a service (SaaS) technology to global FMCG brands, but collects the 12 months' license fees upfront at the beginning of each year, thus adding the full year's revenues for the customer to the bank balance. I typically try to get customers to pay for trials so that all of our costs associated with the sale are covered by the customer.

Scale on a variable cost/project basis

I have raised money in businesses where we had too much money: it leads to hiring people and buying resources that we simply did not need. If you decided tomorrow to hire 10 more people, I can guarantee you that, within a few weeks, they will all be busy – even if you have no requirement for them at all.

If you are trying to scale your business and you need certain skills to help you deliver on the plan, try to buy them in as part-time skills from a consultant or an outsourced company. For example, get a professional to provide HR services on a one-day-a-week basis; get marketing skills from a consultant who has more than one client; or hire engineers with particular skills as you need the skills for specific projects. Outsourcing allows you to scale up and down and switch skills as the business requires.

In my own business today, I hire people as part-time workers or consultants, doing a part-time job by the hour or by the day – and only when I really need them. This creates great focus on the skills they have, the role they play and the tasks you assign to them as everything is task-focused and paid accordingly.

Try to be project-based in matching your finances to the resources and costs that are required to deliver your operations. When I owned Nautique, the aftershave company, I outsourced all of the manufacturing, so when I needed more product they put the aftershave on their production line and made it for me. And when I had no demand for product, I was not paying them anything. After time, the risk for your supplier gets smaller as you become more predictable in terms of your customers' commitments and your cashflows.

Avoid family and friends for funding

In a recession where investment is difficult to find, some CEOs resort to their friends and family as a source of growth capital. I have never done this in my career for three reasons:

- First, you need to be absolutely sure of your business success because the stress of looking at these people across the table at Christmas, when things are going wrong, is more than the average person can handle;
- Professional investors in later rounds don't like family and friends on board, because it means lots of small minority investors to deal with as they restructure finances as the business grows;
- And last, if you are focused on really accelerating the growth of your business, you need to think big in terms of finance. Big investors get this. They take risks; that is their business. If it fails, they move on to their next project and play the numbers game in terms of the wins and losses – which brings you back to point one!

15: Funding Accelerated Growth

Avoid selling professional services (or at least plan an exit)

Many companies sell professional services/consulting in the early days of their business growth to help fund the increasing operating costs, but this can be a huge risk to growing your business.

Investors don't put any value on professional services for certain types of business. They want to see software revenues as a monthly commitment for x number of years – they know that this is where the real value lies. If you are trying to build innovative products or services, while at the same time providing consultancy, there is a constant struggle between what needs to be done for the consultancy part of the business and the core business itself. Often companies cannot separate the two and so ultimately never scale or achieve their business plan.

If you can raise the capital to pursue your business without the need to rely even temporarily on professional services, then that is always the best option. It keeps the focus on creating a valuable and exciting business. But, if you need to provide professional services to make ends meet, make sure you know how to move away from them over time and as the core business grows. Make a plan to do so and stick with it. This is hard to do and takes focused and disciplined management from the top if it is to succeed.

How to capture your funding for accelerated growth in your Accelerated Growth Plan slide deck ...

When you are presenting your finances, it is best to show some clear and simple graphs of both your historic and future revenues, overheads and margins. Outside of this, you can talk about how you propose to fund the accelerated growth: whether you need investors or can fund the business through your customers. If the latter is possible, how will you structure your finance to do so?

16

MANAGING THE BUSINESS

- Keep senior management in-house and outsource everything else
- Do you really need an office?
- Do you really need to travel?
- Open up your internal communications
- Move to the cloud
- Use technology to scale globally
- Use key performance indicators to track progress
- What's the difference between accelerated growth and normal growth?

Your operations are important because ...

How you operate your business is a key part of your overall strategy for successfully accelerating the growth of your business. Getting your operations right can be a huge lever for accelerating growth, while getting it wrong can be a significant blocker to your growth.

Like all aspects of a business today, the market continues to change at a rapid pace, but for me the changes in how I can operate my business, due mainly to the availability of new technologies, has had a significant impact on accelerating the growth of my current business.

Access to cloud-based hosting facilities, that are easy to access and deploy and that are inexpensive relative to traditional dedicated hosting, is probably the single most important change. We can buy as little or as much hosting capacity for our products as we need, deliver them over the cloud, and then pay as we go, based on the capacity that we use.

I also am amazed at how we work today, when I compare it to how we worked some years ago. I have large mobile operator customers in Europe with heavyweight technologies that we need to connect to for delivering our services. Our operations team are based mainly in the UK, our engineers are based mainly in Pakistan and the management team is based mainly in Ireland, yet no one needs to leave their office to integrate to, deploy or operate our technology for customers who can be based anywhere in the world. Years ago, we would have been flying engineers and servers or other pieces of technology all over the world at huge expense, both in terms of the costs of travel and the time involved.

Keep senior management in-house and outsource everything else

It is easier and cheaper now than ever before to operate a business from anywhere in the world to service customers anywhere in the world – a truly global business.

Drucker, the renowned business author, argued that the organization of the future would hire only top executives. All other support services – HR, finance, operations, engineering, sales – in fact, everything below the senior management team would be outsourced to third party organizations on a pay-as-you-use model. Today, this is happening in businesses all over the world.

I have embraced this model: all of our non-core activities have been outsourced to third parties – for example, all of our engineering function is outsourced to a company based in Pakistan. I do have a small number of resources based locally and employed by the company but this is more for

16: Managing the Business

division of responsibilities to make sure that there is no single point of failure should something go wrong.

Every function in a business can be outsourced. The key to a company's success is the innovation and execution that comes from good senior managers who know how to execute their tasks and to manage resources effectively so everything works in harmony with the overall vision of the business and the senior managers.

Do you really need an office?

Bringing everyone to an office every day is unnecessary in today's world. It is a very outdated idea that many CEOs hold on to because it is what they are used to. I would go as far as saying that some CEOs like to see their employees working or have a fear of them not working if they cannot be seen. I have gone to the other extreme of not having an office that everyone can go to every day; everyone in my current business works from home, with the exception of the engineering team who need to work together because of the nature of their work.

For me – and for many people – commuting time can run close to three hours per day. Multiply this by five days a week and that's 15 hours – almost two days of work per week. Roll this idea across all of your workforce and do the math. Then find a way to allow your people to work remotely – and watch your productivity soar!

I recently built an office in my garden at home. It is designed to be a 'Think Tank' for facilitating strategy sessions – so there are large couches, whiteboards, a kitchen for in-house dining and a boardroom for group meetings. Because my management team is global and we address a global market, they are based in different locations. Every few weeks, I bring them together to agree on the next round of tasks and to review progress. This offsite strategy session keeps everyone focused on the job at hand. And, if someone can't travel for whatever reason, they dial in by conference call. We look forward to these sessions, cover a lot of ground and agree the overall schedule of activities for the business with all the actions that each person needs to complete. By bringing everyone together, updating them on the overall progress and getting each senior executive to update us on their own area, everyone gets to see what everyone else is doing and we can agree on the joint tasks that need focus as a team.

Do you really need to travel?

For many years I always had to travel to meet a customer face-to-face to show them a demo of our online service. Today, I can do this from the comfort and convenience of my home office. I do travel when necessary and in particular to build the initial relationship, but then everything else can be done remotely.

I recently did a presentation and a full demo of our new CRE service to the senior management team of a mobile operator where their entire team was sitting in their boardroom in a different country. We beamed my PC screen onto their screen. I was in Ireland, my sales guy was in the UK and our Head of Engineering was in Pakistan. And we walked them through a full presentation and demo remotely. Before this, it would have cost me several thousand euro just to be at that meeting to get the initial feedback on whether our service was of interest or not. Now we don't need to spend any money to get that initial feedback; so before we start jumping on planes to make the sale, we know we have an interested prospective customer.

If they are interested in becoming a customer, we could move from demo to trials, then to contracts and finally to live service, without ever needing to leave my office. This is one good aspect of working in a recession: your customers don't expect you to spend scarce resources on travel, particularly if they think they will end up paying for it, which ultimately they will.

Open up your internal communications

A huge challenge in every business is internal communications: how can you keep everyone informed and make sure everyone shares ideas and can ask questions to help keep the entire team working in line with the business objectives?

For years, I had the typical office layout where all the engineers and operations people sat in an open plan office, while the senior managers had glass offices looking out onto the floor. The argument is that this layout promotes open communications where anyone can talk to anyone about anything. But think about what happens in practice: if an engineer wants to check a requirement, they must stand up from their desk, walk past all of their peers and colleagues and into the CEO's office to ask a simple question. If they did this, everyone would be wondering what was all that about, what did the engineer and CEO talk about, why did he go to the CEO, etc so it never happens.

Since I adopted our new work practice where everyone works from home, we all use Skype to communicate and my communications with everyone in the company are infinitely better. Every engineer in the team feels empowered to send a quick IM if they see I am online or to make a quick Skype call if it is a more complex issue – and we can agree on a way forward quickly. For my business, where we use agile programming, this has become a powerful competitive advantage: we communicate so well that we get things right first time every time because everyone is empowered to communicate openly with everyone else in the business.

Move to the cloud

In terms of operating a business the cloud and software as a service offer not only cost savings but also the ability to access and use these systems from any device, on any network, from anywhere in the world.

For example, today I can use an online accounting system to create an invoice, add a purchase invoice, record a payment or run my management accounts from anywhere. I can access my banking service online and pay bills from anywhere. I store all of my files on the cloud so again I can access them from anywhere, share them with anyone and collaborate with them to get shared documents completed. I do my payroll from a cloud system, where again all of the hard work is done by the software and because it is cloud-based, there is no need to update the software when the Revenue changes the rules. Also the Revenue has adopted these technologies to allow companies to file returns and make payments online, taking all the laborious hours of wasted time out of the process.

Today, all of our customer platforms can be deployed and managed by any of our staff from anywhere in the world. At the same time, we can guarantee better service level agreements (SLAs) and better response times to our customers.

The reporting of key performance indicators also is easier with cloud/SaaS tools. For example, our own platforms send weekly Excel reports with key performance indicators (KPIs) of our trading and technical performance to each of the senior management team, saving them the hassle of having to log in and look for this information.

If you are not already using these technologies, you should start to evaluate them because they can have a significant impact on your ability to accelerate your growth – and as you grow, you can scale the technologies in line with your growth.

Use technology to scale globally

Technology can be embraced to help scale any business.

I went on a fishing trip with my father to a remote part of Ireland. We could not help but notice the number of retail stores, restaurants, hotels, etc. that were closed and we both wondered how businesses can survive in such remote locations. When we arrived at the fishing destination, we met our guide who told me that he inherited a business from his father that supplied fishing accessories to fishermen. His grandfather had started the business: he sold to local fishermen. Then his father took over and sold to local and UK fishermen. When our guide took over, he started to source his accessories in China and sold them on the web, so now people from all over the world can buy from him. When they place an order, his system in his shed at home prints off a UPS label with the customer's address, he boxes the product and calls UPS when he has a batch ready for delivery. UPS comes to his home and off the order goes to a satisfied customer. His business reaches markets that his grandfather couldn't even dream of reaching – all from a shed in a remote location in Ireland. And by the way, the money is in his account before the products are shipped to a customer: what a business model! It really drove home to me the scale of the opportunities for companies to accelerate their growth by accessing markets anywhere in the world from anywhere in the world with little or no resources other than a PC connected to the internet.

I met another business that, for years, had manufactured branded clothing for large corporations like the police force and the postal services. The business was based in Europe and very labor-intensive. The old business model was under pressure as new companies from China were able to reach out to European customers and supply direct for a fraction of the cost. So they decided to reach out to smaller enterprises that ordered smaller runs of branded clothing. To do this effectively, they built a web shop-window where customers could design their own clothing online and pay for it. They found their own outsourced supplier in China and spent time and money integrating their web shop-window into the Chinese factory's operations, automating the process from purchase all the way through manufacturing and delivery logistics. Because they understood the value chain of collecting the requirements and delivering the finished goods, they were able to automate the complete process while getting out of manufacturing at the same time.

Some years ago, you had to invest heavily in a call center to support customers who bought your products and services. Today, depending on the type of business you run, you can provide self-help tools such as reporting online or self-service access to your services to switch on or off whatever the

16: Managing the Business

customer wants to buy. It is now so easy to record a video that walks a customer through your software-based service, load it onto YouTube, link it to your website or service and let the customer do the rest.

Other companies are starting to leverage the web to get outsiders to offer support for their products for free – for example, if you supply an online service and people love it, they are often willing to tell others how to enjoy the service. Blogging is a great source of fixing technical problems. These are real people – your customers – who are prepared to give up their time for free just to help someone else to enjoy your service. If your business has always relied on call center support, just think how you could scale your business and your bottom line if you could generate this form of free support!

Use key performance indicators to track progress

You may have heard the saying, "What gets measured gets done." I am a great believer in tracking all aspects of the business using KPIs or metrics for the key drivers of success of your business.

The KPIs that I track are daily sign-ups for our service, activation rates, usage across all services and revenues; the report is less than one page. Once I see these KPIs, I know exactly how we are scaling. I share these KPIs with the senior management team so they also know how well we are performing; everyone knows that new customers and more usage drives more revenues, so we are all aligned with the overall company objective.

In the past, when I operated from an office with all the team in one place, I used digital signs throughout the business to flash up the KPIs for the business so everyone could see how we were doing. When I was running a sales team, I kept a scoreboard on the wall for everyone to see what progress the team was making – or their lack of progress, in some cases.

If this is the culture that you promote in the business, then people are happy to work with it. Over time, it keeps the focus on what needs to be achieved and everyone is kept informed of progress. If you are starting to scale and the numbers are looking good, it is a huge motivator for everyone in the business to drive their performance to reach the targets that are set.

What's the difference between accelerated growth and normal growth?

I was asked by someone "How do you know when a company is experiencing accelerated growth and not just normal growth?." For me, the difference is very clear – but I think you have to experience it to know it. It's like the turbocharger kicking in on the engine of a high-powered car, or the final acceleration of a plane before it takes off.

Most companies grow slowly and add incremental sales month on month, with revenues growing gradually over time. It can all feel like hard work, every day of the week, without any let up in terms of effort. Many companies never see accelerated growth – they grow slowly with huge effort and most hit a ceiling that they can never break through.

Accelerated growth is when you cannot cope with the customer orders that are flowing into the business. You are yourself always under pressure – a different type of pressure – managing all of the resources of the business and bringing in new resources all the time to meet the overwhelming customer demand for your products or services. There is a great sense of excitement in the business, as you win more and more market share; your competitors are watching you and wondering how you are doing it; you eventually leave the field of competitors behind and it feels like you are unstoppable. Accelerated company growth is the image on the front cover of this book, the racing yacht as it planes through the ocean riding the crest of a wave, with all of the team and the captain working in perfect harmony – and having a ball in the process.

How to capture your operations in your Accelerated Growth Plan slide deck ...

You want to capture your ability to deliver the business and to scale it in a single slide.

Explain the type of technology that you use, how your operations support customers, how your people work, where they work, etc. You want to give your audience confidence that you can support the current business and continue to deliver a good service as you continue to scale, while doing all of it at the lowest cost for the best possible solutions.

Talk about the basic foundations of your operations that are solid and in place to make sure that you do not fall over as a business or let customers down. But also talk about your innovations in this area as discussed above that can be leveraged to your advantage for scaling the business.

SECTION 3
OTHER CONTRIBUTORS TO ACCELERATED GROWTH

17

MAKING BEST USE OF YOUR BOARD OF DIRECTORS

- A board of directors or an advisory board?
- Be in control of your board
- Managing a VC-appointed board of directors
- Working on the business, not in the business
- How to run board meetings
- How to appoint a board of directors
- How to motivate board members

Your board of directors is important because ...

Having a good board of directors who are active in the strategic planning and monitoring of the business can be a significant asset to accelerating a company's growth – in fact, it is almost essential.

A board has a statutory obligation to manage the business on behalf of the various stakeholders (shareholders, employees, suppliers, etc) so it serves a very important and practical function.

The board should be the sounding board for all strategic decisions. They should be able to assist in the development of high level plans that can give a company a competitive advantage over others, particularly if they have specific industry experience. They should have contacts that can be leveraged by the CEO and other senior management for the benefit of the company. They will bring a discipline to the reporting and supervision of the company that outsiders expect. For example, if you are approached by a larger company that wants to buy your company, they will know that your company is well-run when they see a good board in place. I have seen acquirers walk away from good companies that they were going to buy, because the company did not have a board that could show a level of control that gave the potential acquirer comfort that everything had been managed well.

Many of the bad stories about the value of a board center on the CEO being forced to take on board members, who then impose a huge burden on the CEO's time in preparing for and managing regular board meetings that feel like an additional overhead to the business. This typically happens when you take on venture capital for the first time and a non-executive board member (or more than one) is imposed on you by the VC to supervise their investment and to make sure that you are delivering the plan that they invested in. In many instances these board members are professional investors, not businesspeople, which can cause friction if the CEO feels that they do not add value to the strategy or running of the business. However, before such board directors are appointed, many CEOs only complete the bare minimum in terms of statutory forms, minutes of meetings, resolutions, etc, but these become very important as you scale the business, so board meetings drive this discipline and give great structure to the company.

I would advise any CEO who is accelerating the growth of their company to get a good board in place. I typically start to appoint expert board members to the company when all the start-up work is done and the company is beginning to scale. A good board can be the best spend of money by a CEO in a company that wants to grow, if you can get the right level of experience by your side.

A board of directors or an advisory board?

A member of a board of directors has a large and growing set of legal obligations to the company and to third parties who work with the company. It is much more difficult to get a good non-executive director (NED) to work for a small start-up company, because of the fear of the company failing and the implications of this for the person involved. These include restrictions from practicing as a director for several years and, in extreme circumstances, personal liabilities if they are found to be negligent in their role as a NED. So it is a serious decision for a NED to take on the role. I have been asked to join the board of a number of start-up companies, but to date I have not accepted any of the offers due to the potential risk of these companies failing and the implications for me as a person who owns and operates my own company. The more established a company is, the easier it can be to recruit well known and experienced board members.

If you find that appointing a statutory board member is proving too difficult, consider an advisory board, which consists of industry experts, often the same people that you would appoint to your board, but acting only in an advisory capacity and thus avoiding the legal obligations that membership of a board of directors entails.

Some companies do both: they build out the main board with NEDs and also appoint experts who would not otherwise join the board to an advisory board. If you do this, beware of the potential for conflict between the roles of the two boards and also the fact that an advisory board can inadvertently take on statutory obligations if it is not properly appointed and managed.

Be in control of your board

A board can be a huge resource to a CEO but, to make it work, you must be in control of who is appointed to it. I would advise any CEO that is accelerating their company growth to start appointing board members as soon as they begin to scale the business. Don't wait to be forced to do this by a VC – start the process yourself as early as possible so, by the time you are forced to take in NEDs on behalf of investors, you already have a well-functioning board with people who are adding value all the time.

Many start-up CEOs appoint their life partner or their business partner as a board member at the time of the company's incorporation, simply because there is a statutory obligation to have a minimum of two directors, so you grab the nearest person without thinking about the longer term impact of this decision. As the company grows, it often makes sense to remove these people as board members and to add more experienced people from industry who will add more value to the company through their attendance at board meetings and their external connections.

Another benefit of appointing your own board early is that you have people that you know and trust, who work with you based on their expertise in an area that maybe you are weaker in and who are there to support you and help you to succeed.

Managing a VC-appointed board of directors

When a board member is forced on you by a VC, you may not get the benefits outlined above, if you raise a significant round of investment and have more than one VC, they may appoint a number of board members who are all coming from the same place in terms of their drivers. By having an existing team of board members that you have appointed yourself and that are firmly on your side, it can help tip the balance of power in your direction.

VCs often make good NED appointments – no less experienced or as good as your own appointees – but typically VC-appointed directors are there to serve the VC, to protect their investment and this can drive different agendas at times. When everyone is focused on the success of the company and accelerating its growth, there is alignment of objectives – however, when things go wrong, you can quickly see a divide in the objectives. Remember that, when the board represents the majority of the shareholdings in the company, then as CEO you work for them not the other way around. So if they don't think you are up to the job of accelerating the growth of the company, or things take a turn for the worse, you could find the board going against you and you yourself getting fired from the company that you created. I have seen this happen and, in each case, the CEO/founder is shocked – but it does happen.

Working on the business, not in the business

A good board can have a significant impact on the growth of a business by forcing the CEO to work *on* the business and not *in* the business. This is one of the single greatest failings of CEOs who are trying to accelerate the growth of their company: they are always working in the business, caught up in the detail of looking after an important customer while forgetting the bigger picture, like how to win the next customer.

When I started my accountancy practice, Dowling & Co, I had one important client, but as a single client they did not pay me enough to grow the business and I found myself working for them all day every day because I was the only person in the practice. But I knew that, if I did not hire another person to do this work, even though I did not have the money to do so at the time, my business would fail to grow. So I went to my bank, got an overdraft and hired another chartered accountant to do this work and, because I now had an even bigger problem with my cashflow, I had to go out and find new customers. I did and the practice grew very fast because I kept doing this. I rarely got very involved in any particular client's work: I took the 'helicopter view' and constantly worked on the business, always out winning new customers, speaking at conferences, supervising work, etc.

A good board will always take a helicopter view: they do not want to get involved in the detailed running of the company; instead, they want to see the bigger picture and to track your progress against major milestones. This can be a huge benefit to you as a CEO particularly if you have regular monthly or quarterly board meetings. You will find that you need to think and prepare to justify what you have been doing to accelerate the growth of the business – at a strategic, not a detailed, level.

How to run board meetings

I have learned – from experience – that, to run a good board successfully, you need to manage and prepare for board meetings. CEOs who don't do this do not get the value from their board meetings and end up with a very frustrated board.

A good chairman will help you to plan and prepare for board meetings. If you don't have a chairman like this then I would suggest that you follow these simple steps:

1. Make sure that board meetings are scheduled in everyone's diary well in advance (at least six months) and the time and venue are agreed.
2. Prepare your board pack a few days in advance of the board meeting and send it to the members.
3. At the beginning of the board meeting, take care of the statutory obligations such as appointing auditors, signing off accounts, bringing in further investment, appointing new board members, etc.
4. Read and agree the board minutes for the previous board meeting and get the chairman to sign them.
5. Start the meeting by presenting a summary of the entire board pack. Do this without any interruptions from the board so they know everything that is coming up in the detailed pack.

6. Then walk through the pack but focus on the important areas first while covering all areas before you finish.
7. Ask for the board's feedback, suggestions, help, etc and then manage this. I typically use task-based notes where a task is noted and assigned to members and they must complete it or report back by the next board meeting.
8. Get the basics right: the room, the coffee, the food (if it's a long meeting), projectors, handouts, etc.
9. Don't ever surprise your board – check everything that might be difficult with key board members before the board meeting.
10. Try to manage the time and get decisions made, cover topics briefly, keeping it high level but be prepared to get asked for the detail.

Some CEOs like to do all the board presentation on their own; others prefer to call in their senior management for their section only, like Head of Engineering for Engineering section. This is up to you, but if you bring in your team make sure they are well-briefed and that they leave when they are finished. If they are not experienced enough to present well, then don't bring them in. Many companies bring their CFO or Head of Finance to take minutes of the meeting and they stay for the full meeting.

A good board pack will cover all the important areas of the business. One updated Accelerated Growth Plan slide for each section would form the basis of a good board pack.

How to appoint a board of directors

You need to know what you are looking for in a board member. Typically, you want the person to have a lot of experience in the industry you are in or at least in business, running a company that has had the level of success that you aspire to.

Ideally, you want them to have very specific expertise and experience in an area that you need to know more about to be successful. So, for example, if you are in the medical devices business, you would want a board member who was a senior executive in a company that bought and distributed medical devices all over the world. Or if you are making software for the insurance industry, you would want a board member who ran a large insurance agency and used this type of software so that they know what the issues are for your target customers and so on.

When building out your board, try to get people with complementary skills – someone who understands your market, someone who understands your customers, someone who understands finance, etc. Also try to plug your own personal weaknesses, so if finance is not your best skill and you cannot afford a CFO, bring in a NED with good corporate finance skills.

Needless to say, there are recruitment and executive search agencies ('headhunters') that specialize in sourcing NEDs but they can be expensive in terms both of cost and your time. In my experience, if you know your industry well, you can track down the type of people that you want through people you already know. Typically, they will be veterans of the industry, with years of experience behind them and time to sit on your board. People who are professionally qualified as directors can be good on the statutory side of managing the board but, in my experience, most CEOs go for the industry-experienced individual with or without the professional board qualifications.

How to motivate board members

If you want the best board you can get, then you need to know how to motivate them to join your team and to work for you. A good board member will pick and choose the appointments that best suit their own agenda. They won't take risks with their reputation if they think there is any chance of you failing and will ask a lot of hard questions before agreeing to take up an appointment.

One of the most important aspects of motivating a NED to join your board is your ability to inspire them with your vision. Every NED wants to be part of something great, but in particular the best NEDs are the people with the most experience and who often have more money than they need so, for them, being inspired by the vision of the company is critical to motivate them to join your Board. For example, you may have created technology that can revolutionize the industry that they have worked in all their lives and this is what motivates them to be on your team, not the money and often not even a shareholding. CEOs are often amazed at this: that a brilliant NED would work for nothing – but they do, if you can inspire them enough.

More typically, a NED gets paid an agreed salary *per annum* for an agreed number of days – effectively a good consulting day rate. If the company is early stage, some NEDs will take shares instead of pay – anything from 5% of the company to a double digit number if they have something significant to contribute. I typically offer share options that only get vested as the company succeeds, so the NED is rewarded for their contribution and not the hope of their contribution.

You almost always cover their expenses, such as flights and accommodation and you always pay for their meals out (at least, I always got stuck with the bill on a night out with the board!). If you have VC-appointed NEDs, the VC may charge the company a management fee that covers the cost of the board member.

18

WORKING WITH VENTURE CAPITALISTS

- VC money can be expensive
- Do VCs add strategic value?
- Know the business profile of your intended VC
- Get references for a VC from other entrepreneurs
- Always raise VC money when you don't need it
- VCs are investors (not your friends)
- Keep your VC honest – always have a competitor close by
- Is the money or the entrepreneur more important for success?
- When it is time to step down as CEO

Venture capital is important because ...

Venture capital can add huge and essential value to your business if you want to accelerate its growth. Some businesses simply could not exist – let alone scale – without venture capital support. One venture capitalist (VC) I know describes venture capital as the 'rocket fuel' for growth – this is true when you get everything right; but get it wrong and venture capital can become the most expensive form of capital that a CEO or founder can buy; get it badly wrong and you could find yourself booted out of your own company with no equity and no job, even though the company you have created might have been a huge success.

Being able to access growth capital from VCs can be essential to accelerate the growth of most companies. There can be any number of reasons for needing venture capital, but the most common reason for companies wanting to accelerate their growth is to go faster, so they can capture the market opportunity that exists today or not miss it all together or not lose out to a bigger player who simply copies you. Whatever the reason, being well-funded is a significant advantage in the market.

The level of funding and the risks that the VCs are prepared to take can vary significantly from country to country and from region to region within countries. Although, the US market leads the charge in terms of the amount of capital that is available and the risk profile that its VCs are prepared to take on board, Silicon Valley is in a different orbit from Boston or New York, and the rest of the country trails behind. Although great ideas do come from Europe, generally US competitors raise significantly more money more quickly and thus can win market share early and ultimately dominate – some recent exceptions are (hopefully) a welcome trend. Because these market dynamics are important to know as a CEO, I will talk about them in more detail in **Chapter 20** in the context of exiting your business.

The key advantages of being well-funded are that you get to take a reasonable salary yourself, hire the people you need, get the technology you wanted, travel to customers anywhere in the world and arrive in one piece well-fed and ready for business, etc, as opposed to always bootstrapping.

But there is a difference between early and later stage VC investing. A very different mindset is needed if you are trying to get a company to prove the business model of a technology/ service, etc than if you are trying to achieve global domination on the back of a proven concept. In the first, the company typically needs money and everyone in it should be parsimonious on how it is spent; in the latter, the company has chosen to fuel itself up and the dynamics are very different – and specific for each company.

18: Working with Venture Capitalists

VC money can be expensive

However, there's a downside too: venture capital is not free. In fact, it can be the most expensive money that you will buy as a CEO / founder of a company, but often it is the only money that you can get as a new company accelerating its growth. If you need significant capital to accelerate your growth but you are an early stage company, you will not get the funding you need from other sources such as banks – so the only game in town is the venture capital market. Remember that VC money is high risk/high return. If you borrow money from a bank, you would have to offer your house or first born as collateral; VCs typically invest in equity instruments, not debt, and require no collateral.

When you raise venture capital, you effectively are selling shares in your company. And the VC will want to sell these shares at some stage in the future. So when you raise venture capital, you have started the process of selling your company – albeit piecemeal over time (see **Chapter 19**). The shares you sell to VCs have a value but the earlier the stage of your company, the less valuable they are to a third party investor. Your job is to maximize the value of these shares for the cash that you raise while maintaining control of your business so you can continue to grow it the way you want. Knowing when the right time is to raise venture capital is very important if you want to maximize the value of your equity. Having sufficient proof points that show that the business model is working, the products are working, the market is growing, etc all help hugely in getting a good price for your equity.

Don't forget that VCs are financial investors: typically they want proof points that show how your company can become the next great company. You show this not by making a profit from selling consulting services nor by conserving cash by not investing in the right areas, but by showing that your business model will work. Even though it may not be adding much revenue to the bottom line, your business model must show that customers want to buy your new product or service even though it may not be properly built yet. You must show that you know exactly how to fix an operational issue or a product scaling problem, once you get the cash to do it as opposed to doing it now without the customers. Having too many customers wanting a product or service so that you cannot meet their needs because your company is under-funded is a good place to be when raising venture capital.

I have often heard people say that you should raise as much venture capital as you can when you can, but my advice is to raise only just enough at a good price for your equity. Try to hold back selling too much at this early stage when your equity has a lower value. If you can hold on to your equity, its value will rise as your company grows. Typically in each VC round you sell 20% to 30% of the equity, so it is important to understand how much cash is needed to get your business to the point of financial stability.

I know it is hard to believe but too much money can damage a business. If you lived through the dotcom era you will know what I mean. Too much money can make a company lazy and less focused on winning. You can lose the drive and ambition to succeed if the VC money comes too easy.

Do VCs add strategic value?

When you do the rounds of VCs to raise money with a company that they all want a part of, you can get them to enter a bidding war with one another. Apart from the valuation they offer, VCs will sell themselves to you based on the strategic value that they can add and how they can help you to grow faster through contacts, market knowledge, board members, by leveraging other investments, etc. In my experience, this additional value never materializes and you soon realize that mostly they bring money to the table but little else. Money is fine, but don't expect or buy in to the other benefits that one VC will sell you over the other VCs that are bidding for your equity.

Nonetheless, people do matter, so finding a good VC with good partners that have industry experience is very valuable and can make your life a lot easier. Bringing in a VC who has no experience in your industry can be a significant overhead as you attend board meetings and have to explain everything about your business over and over again. Also having someone that you respect and trust (and ideally that you like working with) can be a significant resource to you in your decision-making by sharing some of the burden.

When you decide to take on a particular VC, make sure you pick the right partner to sit on your board. It is only at the negotiating stage that you get to have a say in this matter so, if you have connected with one of the partners and if they have relevant experience that you can leverage for the benefit of the business, ask for that person to sit on your board. The same goes for any NED that they want to appoint from outside their own team – try to have a say in this matter to make sure that, in addition to the supervisory role that they play for the VC, you get some strategic value from them as a board member.

Know the business profile of your intended VC

Venture capitalists are a business just like yours: the difference is that they buy and sell company equity while you might be selling software. For VCs to be successful, they need to get (much) higher returns on the cash that they have put into your business than they could achieve by putting it on deposit. They need to sell this to the pension funds that give them their funds and they must try to prove that they are better than the next VC at doing this. Unfortunately, in recent times, the VC world has shown to be a very bad investment for many investors, with annual returns in single digits or, in some cases, negative. As a result, some VCs are struggling to raise their own funds because they do not have a compelling business proposition for their own investors.

This has implications for you as the key equity owner. VCs are stock-pickers in illiquid stocks and must pick companies that are going to succeed in giving them a significant return on their investment, enough to cover their losses on the companies that don't succeed, and so they want to put as little funds into play ('bullets' as they sometimes like to call them) for the maximum amount of equity.

If a VC does not have a good-sized fund to follow on from a small initial investment, you could find yourself being locked out of the market for large VCs to come in and raise your value when you need more funding later.

VCs without a good-sized fund can get caught up in trying to:

- Maximize their own position due to their own specific circumstances – for example, trying to get a next round done at a very low value so they get more equity;
- Make the company get to break-even too early;
- Get the company to exit the business to a larger company too soon, so the founder gets little or no return;
- Get the company to generate or spend cash in ways that don't make sense to the long-term value of the business;
- Bring in other forms of investment, such as debt finance, too early or at rates that are damaging to the growth of the business.

If you end up with a VC like this, you could significantly damage your own prospects for growth and, ironically, because you brought in venture capital to accelerate your growth but from the wrong VC, you have limited your ability to grow in the longer term. If you do choose a small(er) VC fund, make sure that they have the experience and drive to work with you and to bring in larger VCs as the company grows, thus becoming true partners in the success of the business.

Get references for a VC from other entrepreneurs

The proverb says: "If you want to know me, come live with me." VCs are all charming and well-intended when you meet them for the first time but they are no different to any other supplier to your business: they have something that they want to sell to you and you have something you want to buy so you need to know whether what they are selling will work for you.

With VCs, the devil is always in the detail. On the surface, they all look and act the same and they try to differentiate themselves by promising to leverage industry knowledge, connections, etc. At the end of the day the product that they sell is the same the world over: they sell cash at a price.

But like any product or service, there can be a significant difference between VCs – in their people, their intent, their behavior, their terms and their ability to help you to be successful.

If you are looking at working with a specific VC, get references from other entrepreneurs who took money from them. It is easy to find out what companies the VC has invested in because they all show their investment companies on their websites or marketing collateral. If you know any of these companies, especially the ones that have exited, go talk to the founders and get their feedback on how the VC acted.

VCs will tell you about all the successful exits and, on the whole, the CEOs/founders of these companies support the successful exit story because we all want to look good and get the newspaper headlines for our success. But the reality can be totally different to the story that is put out to the market. I know entrepreneurs/CEOs who had equity in a successfully exited business but who would say that they got shafted on the way by the VC and ended up with very little for their efforts.

Some VCs can be very fair and generous, believing that it is important to keep the CEO/founder fully motivated and to get them a return for their hard work; others simply don't care and will take as much as they can when the exit comes. You need to be with a VC that gets the bigger picture and wants to create a relationship whereby you as CEO positively refer them to other CEOs, you will go to them for funding for your next venture and they will continue to be good friends and advisers as you continue in your career.

Bottom line: ask around before you do a VC deal and get feedback from current and exited company founders and CEOs.

Always raise VC money when you don't need it

Every experienced entrepreneur who has been through a successful exit with VCs on board will say to you to always raise venture capital money when you least need it, assuming you can get a good value. VCs love to invest in companies that don't need the cash to survive; they want to see their cash being used only for accelerating growth if at all possible. So the ideal company is one that is growing, making sufficient cash to continue funding itself, but could go a lot faster if more money was invested now. Typically, these companies don't need to raise cash but this is the best time for you to raise cash because you can raise larger sums for better valuations. The money you raise can sit in the bank for a rainy day if it is not needed. The best CEOs raise money they don't need, to keep as a cushion if things get tight for some reason but they continue to grow from their own cash reserves generated through trading.

Don't ever wait until you are nearly out of cash to raise funding and don't rely on your existing VCs to give you great terms if you are about to run out of cash, particularly if you are not meeting your business plan that they bought into so you are running out of cash earlier than originally planned. If you do this, expect to take a bath in terms of the amount of equity you will give up – they will give you a rock bottom price if you let them.

So always raise money well before you need it, regardless of your existing VC's advice.

VCs are investors (not your friends)

Recognize that VCs are professional investors whose job it is to find great companies like yours and, when they do, to buy as much equity as possible for as little investment as possible and then to grow and to exit the business as fast as possible.

Once you know that these are the rules of engagement, you can anticipate them and manage the relationship. But don't get led down the path by your new 'best friend'. They have a job to do and it's not personal when they do it; but you also have a job to do and you need to make sure also that it is not personal.

It is often advisable to have a middleman (your corporate lawyer is often a good choice) to negotiate with your VCs, as these deals can get very stressful, and so entrepreneurs who tend not to want to fight with their investors give in to their demands. VCs don't like dealing with middlemen and it costs you money that you may not have but, if there is serious money involved and serious equity being given up, make sure you have someone to fight your corner.

There's lots of information on the web about what VCs typically look for in terms of clauses and how they manage these, but watch out for hidden clauses and clause changes. VCs love to bog you down in lengthy contracts that they change over and over again and again until they wear you down and you sign for things that you never expected to agree. You simply cannot afford to pay a lawyer to read these changes over and over again because it is so expensive, so typically you end up reading the contracts yourself at night at home with your partner and kids wanting your time – and you fold. Don't do this. Be firm on what you want from the outset and be prepared to walk away.

If you get this wrong, you can find yourself stripped of all the equity in the company you founded and worked so hard to build – and even without a job. I know too many cases where this happened. Remember: VCs are investors – not your friends.

That said, I have been lucky to work with some great VCs, people who are still my friends to this day. I respect their expertise and experience and call them for advice from time to time. The relationship with a VC can last up to seven or even 10 years – longer than some marriages. Like any relationship it must be developed – it's not just a commercial transaction – and requires time and effort from both parties.

Keep your VC honest – always have a competitor close by

As the CEO of your company, you need to keep open lines of communication to potential investors outside of your existing VC investors as you grow your company and move towards later-stage funding. If you don't continue to deal with third party investors, you will struggle to keep your existing investors honest and, over time, they will dilute you faster and more than you will believe.

Typically, when an investor comes in, they push you to grow the business and to stay focused on this. That's good advice – but it also means you are too busy to find new investors. They assure you that they will continue to support the business and will do a follow-on investment when it is needed, but by the time you come to discussing the new investment round you have run out of time to bring in a third party investor so you leave yourself exposed to taking a bath for a list of spurious reasons from the VC as to why they are keeping the value low and taking more equity from you for the next round, usually blaming you for not achieving the plan they bought into (which by the way happens in 90% of cases). You must continue to manage your current investors and always look to bring in third party investors to keep some tension on your VCs and to ensure the best price for your equity.

18: Working with Venture Capitalists

What this means is that, the day after you take in VC money, you start to plan for the next round of investment – not from this VC but from another. Once you have another on the hook, then you can negotiate with your current VC; otherwise, you have no negotiating position.

And by the way, if you do talk to third party VCs, don't tell your existing VC who you are talking to. Keep them in the dark while you have control of your own business.

Is the money or the entrepreneur more important for success?

I have often heard a CEO state that they are so critical to the businesses that the VC-controlled board could never fire them. It is a mistake to believe that VCs think that you are completely indispensable – many VCs believe not only that you are replaceable but often that your replacement will do much better as a CEO. I would argue that the vision, passion, leadership and gut instinct that has got you to where you are today can bring you all the way and it is often far more important to the success of a company than the skills of a so-called professional CEO. But not all VCs get this or believe this; sometimes they are right but, from the CEO's side of the fence, I would argue that they are more often wrong than right about this.

I remember a conversation with a partner from one particular VC in Europe where we got in to this specific argument and he argued that the most important element in creating a successful company was the cash. Needless to say, I argued robustly that the most important component is the entrepreneur with the idea, the vision, the passion, the leadership, etc to bring a company to success. Neither of us won the other over but both of us came away with a new perspective.

Another VC friend of mine answered the riddle for me by telling me that there are three legs to the successful company stool: one is the entrepreneur; the second is the cash; and the third is having something that is compelling in a growing market. I have to admit that I agree with him; you need all three legs for the stool to stand, the difference is that some companies can generate their own cash to accelerate their growth through trading while others need to raise it from VCs.

But my key message is to be realistic about your own power. If you have a VC or a group of VCs who now have a controlling stake in your business, you now work for them and you need to perform or they will look to replace you. Because all is fair in love and war as they say, a VC needs to make sure the company is as successful as it can be and, if you are not seen to be helping in this process or even blocking it, they will take you out.

When it is time to step down as CEO

At some point, a good VC may point out that the time has come for you to step down as CEO if you want your company to reach the levels of success that are possible for it to achieve. By the time this happens the VC or your board will have had a good opportunity to witness your abilities as a CEO and they are often right to suggest that it is time to step down.

With a good VC on board you should be perfectly aligned in terms of what success looks like; if you have worked very hard to get the company to where it is now and you want to get a good exit yourself, then you want to see your company do as well as it can possibly do. Your skills have already been proven; you may have created a new idea and brought it to market; you have built a team to get this far but maybe the company now needs more skills and experience than you have to give in areas like HR, operating support systems, accounting and finance, large scale production, customer call centers and support, etc.

If you think your business can be more successful with a new CEO, then be prepared to step down because the reward is a better return on your own investment. If you are working with a good VC, they will accommodate you and keep you in the senior management team if you need the salary or use you for your best skills like strategy or innovation. They also will keep you on the board of the company so you can contribute to the high level decisions as the company goes forward. And your people will continue to respect you as the founder of the company, looking for your advice and support as usual but also knowing that there is a new CEO who makes the final decision.

It often can be a great relief for a founder CEO to step down and let a more experienced CEO take over. It lets you get out of the firing line and allows you to step back to do what you enjoy doing while still being part of the successful company that you created.

But it's a major change – for you personally, for your team and for the company. The change needs to be handled well on all sides if it is to work.

19

SELLING YOUR COMPANY

- Companies are bought not sold
- You can position for sale
- Plan to go 100 times faster
- Get all governance issues sorted
- Secure company IPR
- How to value your company
- What professional advice do you need?
- The selling process
- Listing your company on a stock exchange

Selling your company is important because ...

If you have taken on venture capital, then by definition you are on a path to sell your business. A VC must get a return on their investment in your company and the only way that this can happen is if they sell the company (or list it on a stock exchange). So a VC's agenda, post-investment, is to grow the company as quickly as possible with a view to exiting it within say three to five years. In some cases getting to an exit can take a lot longer, but when you get to the 10-year mark a VC will want to offload your company to get their cash back into the fund so they can close it and show a return to their own investors. If they have had a few good wins with other companies by the time they get to exiting yours, they can be prepared to sell at any price just to get their investment back and close the book on it. So selling your company is a part of your Accelerated Growth Plan if you have a VC on board.

If you don't have a VC on board and you still own the majority of your shares, selling your company also can be an important part of your overall strategy – for example, if you think the market will pass you by due to being undercapitalized, or simply because larger companies also can see the market opportunity and can take the market from under your feet when they point their resources towards it, or because the opportunity to sell is here and now and the market dynamics are right for you to maximize the return on your own investment.

The last point is critical: timing is everything. I know a company that boomed in the early 2000s. It was in a fast-growing market, with great products that made great margins, and the founders owned 100% of the company. It was so successful that VCs wanted to take a stake and give the founders all the cash, which they did for a small stake in their company. They got several offers to sell the business but, because the company was making so much money, they refused to sell and held out for a bigger return. The million or so that the founders received from the sale of the minority stake to the VC was soon spent and the market passed them by as major technology companies became the dominant players; sales fell and the company went from employing hundreds of people to just a handful; today, the founders are only scraping a living. They should have sold the business when the market was hot. When a wave comes, you need to ride it and maximize the return that you can get. If the market is too hot and you know that others will eventually dominate, then you need to know when to take the money and run.

Markets move from early stage, to proven and growing to maturing. Once a market has been proven by a smaller company like yours, larger companies buy their way into the market because it is easier and faster to do this than to start from scratch. Hence mergers and acquisitions (M&A) become very active at a certain point in the growth of a market and, when it does, you need to make a decision to sell or hold. Remember the line in Kenny Rogers' song, *The Gambler*: "You've got to know when to hold them, know when to fold them, know when to walk away and know when to run." There is a time to hold and a time to sell if you want to make a good return on your investment.

Companies are bought, not sold

Companies are bought, not sold. In other words, if you wake up tomorrow, decide to sell your company and appoint professional advisers, it is very unlikely that you will sell your company or, if you do, you will get a rock-bottom price for it.

This sometimes happens when your VC investor needs to get their money back from your investment because a fund is closing or they are trying to raise their own new fund and need to show their returns. Typically, they appoint professional advisers to sell the company, but the results and the process can be very disheartening for you and your senior management who may have no say in the process other than to 'put up and shut up' as they say.

Another reason for putting the company up for sale is the prospect of running out of cash or some other major event that could cause the downfall of the company – again the prices that can be achieved in a distressed sale are bad because you are over a barrel.

This happened to me with imagine. We lost a court case that allowed our supplier to pull their contract that supplied us with airtime (the ability to connect calls on a mobile phone). Without this, we could not supply our service to our customers, so we had only a few weeks to sell our business to another mobile operator. We did manage to sell it but, as you can imagine, the price was rock bottom relative to the real value of the business at the time.

You can position for sale

You can position your company for sale and remain in control of the exit process, as long as you do not have an overriding reason to sell.

Once you get past the start-up stage and the company is a little more established and starting to accelerate its growth, you should begin to think about positioning it for a sale if this is something that you must do because you have VC investors on board or because you want to achieve a good exit for yourself and your other shareholders.

There are a number of ways to attract a good buyer over time:

- **Create a reseller partnership with a larger company that can sell your products and services to their larger set of customers:** If they see the potential in your products or services, they could buy your company to keep all the profit for themselves;
- **Make your service strategic to another company:** Either through partnering or by supplying them with products or services that help them to be more strategic themselves. So, for example, if your product drives new customer engagements because it opens doors, then your partner could use it to sell more of their core products or services;
- **Deliberately upset your larger competition by targeting their key customers and winning business from them:** The more you do this, the more they will notice you. Eventually, they will react in one of two ways: either they will squash you competitively or they will buy you to take you out of their market, particularly if you are too disruptive and risk undermining their existing business model;
- **Create products or services that your competition want to get their hands on, due to the intellectual property, innovation or business model you are using, once you have a few large and important customers on board:** Again you must make sure that your potential acquirer gets to hear about this;
- **Put your company out there as a market leader by making a lot of noise at trade shows, speaker events, in the press, on other PR media, etc:** If you make a lot of good noise, a potential acquirer is more likely to hear about you, but it should all be focused on the success of your growing business and not on shouting "We're For Sale."

Plan to go 100 times faster

When you are thinking about selling your company, you should plan to be able to go 100 times faster than you are going today. In other words, if you are selling your company to a larger company, typically they are buying you to put your product or service into their existing customer base, which by definition is much larger than yours, so make sure when they come to buy you that you can show them how your company can handle 100 times more customers.

Whatever the number is in terms of multiples of scale you need to be able to show the acquirer how you can scale up from where you are today to meet the potential demand that they could bring to your business through their existing customers. You don't need to have the additional capacity in the business today but you must be able to demonstrate how you can put it in place. If you make products this means that your production facility or outsource supplier has the capacity to meet the demand, your operations has the processes to support more customers, your technology has the capacity to scale up based on the underlying architecture that exists today, etc.

I have seen companies that did not prepare for this discussion receive initial expressions of interest from potential buyers, who ultimately walked away once they saw that the company could not scale. So make informed decisions as you put your company resources in place to cater for scaling up and to answer these questions should a potential acquirer come calling.

Just some examples to guide you:

- For a technology company, you can show that the underlying architecture has been designed to allow for scaling up using say load balancing, virtual machines, etc, not deployed today but planned for and easily deployable;
- May be you only operate in English-speaking countries, but how would you handle other languages, how would you support customers in a multilingual call center, is your software ready to show a new language, etc?
- How would you collect cash from another country and get it back to your own currency, how would you employ local people to support customers, do you know the local employment law, what reporting and accounting requirements would you have, etc?

There are many areas that need to be considered in scaling the business beyond your own growth plan, so make sure that you have answers to all of the most obvious questions and that you won't be caught short if you are approached by a buyer.

Get all governance issues sorted

I know this sounds obvious but you would be amazed how many companies don't have the basics in order, simply because they have been too busy fire fighting or because they don't have the rigorous discipline of a larger company. Making sure that customers' contracts are on file, that proper books and records are being kept, that the Companies Office filings are up-to-date, that all employees have contracts of employment, etc are the basics that need to be in place for any business. Don't leave all this until you have been approached to be bought, otherwise vast amounts of the CEO's and the senior managers' time will be needed before you can open up the company to due diligence (a buyer review process to validate that everything you say about the company is as you say on paper).

Some examples of the basics are:
- A good accounting system with monthly management reports;
- Control over invoicing and cash collections;
- Company Office filings are up-to-date;
- Contracts with customers all signed and filed;
- HR files for all employees with contracts of employment;
- Agreed staff review processes and records;
- Reporting systems that show key performance indicators (KPIs) that allow you to track and manage the business;
- Controls over purchasing and banking (who can authorize purchases and payments);
- Share options scheme (if you have one) all documented and in place.

A good way to check whether your company is in order is to make a list of areas that a typical buyer will review when they do due diligence on a company. If you can satisfy all of the items on this list, then you are in good shape to enter discussions with a potential buyer; if not, my advice is to start putting all of these items in place now and then keep them as normal practice, just in case you do get a buyer making enquiries.

Again large companies walk away from buying smaller companies if the paperwork is not in place, because they cannot afford to take risks in terms of unknown liabilities, particularly if they themselves are quoted on a stock exchange.

And if you are serious about selling, consider appointing branded advisers that are known to buyers such as one of the top five accounting firms for your audit; this can give a larger buyer comfort when they look through the numbers.

Secure company IPR

The intellectual property rights (IPR) of a company include its brand, its patented products or software, designs, trade marks, domain names, etc. These are very important assets of your business and they need to be secured and controlled as if they were cash.

Classic IPR mistakes include:
- Registering brands or domains in your personal name and not in the company's name;

- Not filing for protection of IPR (for example, trademarks);
- Not renewing ownership of relevant domain names if they are not actively being used;
- Not protecting your IPR in customer contracts.

You need to have a discipline in your business from the outset to protect and manage these IPR assets. So if you start to use a brand name, make sure that you have done a search on the trade mark and have registered it so you can validly use it – and protect it – not just in your local market but in international markets too.

If you sell software, the IPR requirements are much more onerous. In one company that I sold, I had not done a very good job on securing all the IPR for the software, so we went through a month of backdating contracts with customers, staff, contractors, etc. The deal nearly failed due to this, only that the buyers had worked with me in the past and trusted me I would have never been given the time to get the correct documentation in place and thus, eventually, to get the deal over the line.

For example, if you sell software, every time you engage with a customer you should put in place a non-disclosure agreement (NDA) before you start in-depth discussions. Make sure all of your staff and contractors who worked on building the software have signed over the IPR to the company as potential inventors; this can be covered in their employment contracts, but it must be done. Not doing this can cause a potential buyer to walk away from the deal because of the danger that you may have inadvertently not protected your IPR to the point that there is uncertainty as to ownership.

How to value your company

The golden rule of how much your company is worth is 'what someone is willing to pay'. This is really important to understand, because as much as professional advisers will talk you through the various valuation models, it all depends on how much another company wants to buy your company and how competitive the bidding might be.

There are lots of models that can be applied, such as multiples of revenue, multiples of EBITDA (Earnings Before Interest, Tax, Depreciation and Amortization), discounted cashflows, net assets, etc. But to maximize your valuation, you need to know the strategic value of what you have that the buyer wants to buy.

The most commonly used pricing model is a multiple of your turnover, particularly in a more mature market or where there are larger companies buying smaller companies to grow their own revenues (where the products and service are similar in both companies). Multiples vary from say one times turnover for a well-established, not too exciting business, to say five times turnover for an innovative and fast-growing company. The more established your business becomes and the more akin it is to an established market, then the more likely that you will be valued based on a multiple of turnover that has already been established in the market – it is difficult to get a premium over this number.

Often if a quoted company is offering to buy your company they are locked into a multiple of turnover based on their own valuation and they will be very reluctant to pay much more unless your company can add strategic value to them. So, for example, a large quoted company could signal to the market a move into a new and growing market using your innovations to win new market share; in this case, you can command a much higher price and the acquirer will pay because the market will respond by increasing their own valuation multiple, thus adding significantly more value to their business than the value they have agreed to pay for your company.

To maximize your own value, you need to be able to show growth – ideally, you can prove that the growth achieved was predicted and exceeded; if you can do this, then buyers will accept that your projected growth also will be achieved and thus they will be more willing to pay you more for the higher turnover projected in the future. You will need to negotiate hard for this, but achieving projected growth gives you a good negotiating position.

Knowing the value of what you have that the buyer wants to buy can help you to gain a higher price. So if you know that the buyer has a particular problem that you can solve, or a particular opportunity that you can give them access to, if you can quantify this to the buyer it can help you to put a value, relative to this, on your own business.

Everything in your business has a value – for example, your key people have a value, as do your fixed assets, and even your market location has a value (for example, in Ireland a company can avail of 12.5% Corporation Tax). You need to know the value of all of these assets relative to your buyer – for example, key contracts with strategic customers often can be a reason for one company to buy another; access to new markets (for example, US companies entering Europe) can be a strategic asset to a particular type of company because they can compare this to the cost of establishing their own company in Europe.

What professional advice do you need?

It can be very difficult to sell your own company and get the maximum value possible without the wheels falling off in the process. If, for example, the acquiring company intends to keep you as CEO or as a senior executive, can you have hard-nosed discussions with their senior executives for whom you might soon be working? It can help to have a middleman, or professional adviser, to help you manage the deal. You can blame the middleman for everything when the buyer feels like they are being squeezed to pay more than they want to pay.

These advisers can be expensive and, to some people, it looks like they do very little for the large fee that they receive, but if the deal is a success and you get well-rewarded in the process these fees are irrelevant at the end of the day.

In particular, a good adviser can orchestrate a bidding war for your business between two or more buyers to maximize the value that you receive (note incidentally, in this way, also increasing their own fees). They can do this in a number of ways:

- By approaching similar potential buyers and bringing them to the party;
- By putting pressure on all parties to close a deal by a certain date based on the process;
- By using different selling models to flush out the highest value (term sheets, closed bids, auction, exclusivity in due diligence);
- By having specific industry expertise that allows them to argue the potential growth of your business and the strategic value of your assets.

I know a guy who sold his business some years ago. After an approach from a buyer, he appointed a professional corporate finance adviser to help him sell the business. He wanted an all-cash deal, where he would leave the company. At the beginning of the negotiations, he fronted all the discussions himself but it quickly became apparent that he was stitching himself into the deal and talking too much, to the point of exposing areas of the business that would potentially undermine the valuation. So the advisers took him out of the discussions altogether and put in other senior executives to close the deal. The deal was closed at a much higher value than the CEO set out to attain and he got a lot of cash to simply walk away. Everyone was happy and the buyer got a great company that continued to grow.

Typically, you will need a professional corporate finance adviser: a large bank or a smaller boutique type of private bank, although some large accountancy firms have corporate finance arms that handle sales. You can negotiate to pay on success only; this is easier when there is a buyer already at the table but, if not, the adviser usually asks for a lump sum, a monthly retainer and a percentage of the final deal value, which can be on a downward sliding scale as the value of the deal rises (typically from 5% to 2%).

You also will need a firm of lawyers that knows how to handle a deal like this, writing up shareholders' agreements and managing the various warranties that you may need to give, handling the employment contract if you are staying with the company, etc. It is often best to agree a fixed fee for this type of work as the discussions, contract redrafting and negotiations often tend to go on a lot longer than anticipated.

You also may need input from your existing accountancy firm to make sure that accounts are up-to-date, filings are all done and financial projections are available and understood by the potential buyer – although you should have most of these under control already yourself.

The selling process

If you are going through a sale process for the first time, it can be very intimidating, The fear of the unknown is high, particularly if there is a lot of money involved for you. If you don't have any professional advisers on board, I would strongly advise that you speak to someone who has done this before to get an understanding of what to expect and how to handle the various stages of the sale.

But typically a sale process goes something like this:

- Buyer makes an approach to the company to buy;
- Seller's CEO and senior team provide some high level information (not confidential);
- Seller expresses interest to continue discussions, signs NDA with potential Buyer;
- Seller may appoint professional advisers at this point;
- Seller's CEO and senior team have meeting with Buyer where more detail is shared;
- Both companies share strategic plans for win/win to see whether there is a fit (1+1=3);
- Seller builds senior relationships with Buyer to show they can work together;
- Buyer asked to send term sheet for the deal, showing price that it will pay and how;

19: Selling Your Company

- If term sheet looks acceptable, Buyer can be given exclusivity for a period of time to deal;
- Buyer now allowed access to due diligence files to see specific contracts and company data;
- Seller holds back on trade secrets like software code, recipes, know-how, etc at this stage;
- Seller provides documentation and answers to Buyer on due diligence queries;
- On completion of due diligence, Buyer makes final offer;
- Seller accepts and proceeds to contracts (may need to show trade secrets at this point);
- Buyer and Seller negotiate warranties, senior employment deals, structure of deal, etc;
- Contract for sale and employment contract for CEO closed as deal closes.

The one thing to watch out for in this process for is a lot of politics, particularly if you are controlled by a VC. When you start the deal discussions you work for the VC (if they have a controlling stake), but when you finish you work for the new buyer – somewhere during the process you will switch sides. A lot of tension and politics can build up in a company that is selling between the CEO and the VC, amongst the senior executives and across the business if people are aware of it. You need to be prepared for this and manage it accordingly. Keep a cool head, because where there is a lot of money involved you will see people act in very strange ways. You typically do not tell anyone in the business or outside the business about the potential deal (with the exception of trusted senior management) until it is closed.

You also need to watch out for warranties in your own contract. These are clauses in the contract of sale that allow the buyer to claw back money that it has paid for the company, if it proves at a later stage that you have misrepresented something in the sale process or something was simply not disclosed to the buyer before it closed the deal and that information would have impacted the sale price. The VC often will try to leave you with these warranties, but you need to make sure that they are shared across all shareholders who benefit from the deal and not just you.

Finally it can be difficult to get an all-cash deal from a buyer. Many buyers like to suggest an earn-out, where you get the balance of the deal value only if certain targets are met after the deal is closed. These targets typically are set against reaching sales or profitability that has been forecasted in the sale process on a year by year basis. The rule of thumb for VCs is to discount any earn-out completely from the value of the deal because they rarely get paid (because the targets are not met or reasons to argue against paying it are found after the deal is closed). Again the VC will be happy for you to carry all of the earn-out portion of the deal if they can take all the cash. Make sure that you do not accept an earn-out as part of the core value of the deal, take it as a bonus if you think you can hit the numbers but don't expect to get paid. Focus on the cash and, if you have a VC on board, make sure you get the same deal that they get.

I have so many stories about selling companies but there is just not enough space in this book to tell you all of them (perhaps another book some day?). Suffice to say that the deals you read in the newspaper headlines are rarely as good as they sound and, particularly for the CEO/founder, a bit of advice and experience can help you a lot at this point when all of your hard work is about to get rewarded or not as the case may be.

Listing your company on a stock exchange

For many years the road to success for any CEO and their VCs was to get a company listed on a stock exchange (do an Initial Public Offering (IPO) in US parlance), to get some cash out as the shareholders of the newly-floated company and to raise more cash to further accelerate the growth of the business. But in recent years, this has not been an option because there has been no market for IPOs – like everything in business, the market goes in cycles based on economic conditions – but it will come back and, when it does, you need to take a serious look at it as an option to potentially get some cash out of your business and to raise large sums of cash to grow it further.

When I worked in KPMG as an accountant, I was involved in building the financial models for two companies that were heading for IPO in the 1980s. I remember the hype and excitement of these companies and the process they were going through, where everyone involved was going to receive a big pay-out. These companies were the stars; the founders were in the newspapers every day, drumming up support for their IPO; they were heroes in the business world of that day and I looked up to them.

Getting a company listed is not easy. There is a lot of work involved and a lot of professional fees to pay, but the process has been streamlined with new markets like AIM in the UK and NASDAQ in the USA. The rules for listing and the minimum turnover required etc are all getting easier to meet so I would expect to see the market for IPOs getting stronger and I have no doubt that we will soon see a new appetite for them again.

However, listing has its downside too. A good friend of mine listed his company some years ago and did well in the early days. But then the market for listed companies' shares became very stagnant and his company's share price fell, due to the lack of liquidity (not too many institutions investing in shares), leaving him vulnerable to a takeover at a very low price for the company. In fact, his company was taken over by private investors; they fired him and then stripped out the assets of the company, getting a higher price for its parts than they had paid for the company as a whole. Apart from the fact that he had lost his job and livelihood, it hurt him to see the company that he had spent years building being pulled apart. So it is not all a bed of roses. If you do get your company listed on a stock exchange, you still need to perform well and you need to keep investors interested in your stock – otherwise it becomes hard to raise more cash to further grow the business.

20

BEHAVING ETHICALLY IN BUSINESS

- What is the purpose of your business?
- What is business ethics?
- We need to be able to trust in business
- Capitalism is good
- Consider the public good
- Set company goals that go beyond profits
- Set company values and protect your employees

Business ethics are important because ...

The great thing about writing a book is that you get to speak your mind (whether anyone listens is another matter), but I feel strongly about business ethics and I think it should be included in a book designed to help CEOs to drive the growth of their business.

I was fortunate to be educated by the Jesuits who follow a simple principle of "Educating Men for Others." In everything they teach young boys, they try to instill the concept that, as potential leaders in society, we should always strive to serve others and not just ourselves.

We have all met the type of person who believes that this world was created to serve their needs only and who walks all over anyone who is less well off than them. I once had dinner with one such person, who had made a fortune in business. He sat in London's most expensive hotel, ordering the most expensive food and wines and shouting for service while a table full of guys, like me, looked on. He was big and loud and arrogant. At one point, he said something very inappropriate to the young waitress who was serving us; everyone laughed nervously, but I had enough. I excused myself and said that I was leaving and would not be re-joining him, making it known that I did not approve of his behavior. This guy was a potential investor in my company, but I would never do business with a man like him. Call me stupid if you wish, but when someone has no respect for their fellow man (or woman in this case), he has no integrity and for me this is at the heart of doing business – although I am sure my little protest had no effect on this man.

A business only exists by bringing together a group of people around a common enterprise, so by definition as business leaders we have the choice to serve ourselves or to serve others. I know this sounds very righteous and I also know that we need to serve ourselves before we are in a position to serve others – I think it was Drucker who said "it is difficult to do good until you do well." I can vouch for this; in the early days of Digital Trading, we were doing well and could invest time and money into setting up MyGoodPoints, but then things got tight and we had to pull back – however, as things improve we will be able to focus our resources on doing some good again.

But I believe that we cannot lose sight of business ethics, the simple concept of working and living in a society where we should take into consideration the other people that we will affect with our own business decisions.

20: Behaving Ethically in Business

What is the purpose of business?

Throughout this book, I talk about the many reasons why we start and grow a business but, to look at this from an ethical point of view, do we start a business to serve only our own needs? I would argue not; as a business grows, you bring in more people, who want to contribute their own resources, skills, education, passion, creativity to your business, for their own gain, but also for the benefit of others.

Yes, we need to work to pay our mortgages and to feed and clothe our families, but work is more important that just this. Work gives us a purpose, an outlet for our creativity, a social environment to meet others, a source of pride for our personal achievements, as a team and as a company.

Great companies treat all of their people with respect; they honor them, celebrate their individual successes, support their development and encourage them to grow. These companies make a profit to survive and grow, but the purpose of the business is much wider than the shareholders' needs. It has been proven time and time again that companies that develop and grow their people, through treating them fairly and with respect, achieve much higher levels of performance because their employees believe in the business and what it stands for and this shows when others engage with the business.

I know a very wealthy man who is based in the US, who makes his money by buying up companies, putting them together to grow turnover fast, then floating the whole company off on the stock exchange, taking as much as he can for himself in the process. He never gets involved in the companies he buys, does not meet customers or employees and certainly does not add any value to what they do. He simply sticks them together as quickly as he can, hoping the revenues stay as they are, while he floats the company. He has no respect for his employees, suppliers or his customers – as far as he is concerned, these are only toys in his game of Monopoly. So inevitably the company starts to fail, people lose their jobs and the share price falls, but then he buys the company back at a significantly lower price, delists it, puffs up the revenues again by buying more companies and lists it again on the stock exchange to take many more millions from the unsuspecting public in the process. There is only one person being served in all of this and that is himself. He is hailed as a hugely successful entrepreneur because of his immense wealth. I personally believe that this is unethical business. It is not illegal and there is no law preventing him from doing this, but there is a moral code that we should follow as business people: you don't rip off the general public simply because you were top of your class at corporate finance.

What is business ethics?

Business ethics is about running your business in an honest and fair way with the single most important factor being that you, as the boss, have integrity.

Integrity cuts across all religions, all types of education, and every level of society from rich to poor. Having integrity is probably the single most important ingredient in being an authentic leader. You can make mistakes and go as far as being incompetent, but people will forgive you and still follow you – but if you don't have integrity, people will see through this and will not follow you.

Business ethics is about playing fair and not cheating; it is about not taking an unfair advantage over others just because you can. Twice in my life I had the opportunity to make millions for myself if I was prepared to cheat. Once was a request to make a corrupt payment to gain a huge advantage in business and the second was a wealthy businessman who offered to buy my company if I was prepared to shaft another company that had done a particular deal with me. I said "No" to both. I would have made a lot of money for myself and my family if I had said "Yes," but I would not have slept as easy as I do today and I would have to live with the fact that I cheated in order to accumulate wealth for myself. I was once told by a wealthy (and, in my view, unethical) businessman that I would never be a very wealthy man because I was not ruthless enough – in other words, I would not take advantage of others for my own personal gain. Perhaps so, but I don't believe the two are connected: it's how you get there and what you do when you do that matters.

I brought a senior executive from a very large company out for dinner one night. He insisted on going to a very expensive restaurant, stating "I'll book the restaurant." He then proceeded to order the most expensive meal, outrageously expensive wine and in the process continued to bore the socks off me. But he stiffed me with a huge bill because his own company would not allow this type of expense. He was not overpaid himself and certainly would never spend this type of money out of his own pocket. He took unfair advantage of me simply because he could (at least once). I never did business with this man; apart from his unethical behavior, there were other people in his company that we could and did work with going forward.

When it comes to business expenses, I expect people to do what they would do personally as opposed to moving to a whole new level of opulence just because they can take advantage of the business they work for or get entertained by. I was invited to a party in a restaurant in New York where everyone was drinking the most expensive Dom Perignon as if it were water, so much so that the restaurant ran out of it and we had to move to the most expensive red wine that they had – this was all paid for by the company. Of course, we celebrate our successes and we spend money in the process, but does it need to be the most expensive champagne that money can buy?

We need to be able to trust in business

I always give people the benefit of the doubt and trust them. Sometimes, I have been caught out by giving too much trust but, when trust is broken, as far as I am concerned the business relationship is finished. If you cannot trust another person in business, then in my view you cannot do business with them, or at least you cannot do legitimate and ethical business. I have fired people in the past for stealing from the business; some for minor offences and others for major offences, but big or small I think if someone has the propensity to steal in business then they will do it again, so I simply don't tolerate it in business.

My mother often said to me, "If you understood why people do what they do, you would forgive everyone." She is mostly right and I do always ask for an explanation if I catch someone out, or give them the opportunity to confess, but if the reason is not plausible or they don't own up, then the trust has broken down.

I know that all the great institutions that we trusted all our lives have let us down in recent years: the church, the banks, and the government. The one thing we need to be able to trust is business. We are all educated people in business today, we all make choices in terms of how we want to do business and why we do business, I think we need to take a stand and allow everyone who deals with a professional business person to have trust in them. As business leaders we also have a voice and we have positions of authority over others. We can exercise our influence with all the institutions of the state and rebuild the trust that was once there by getting involved and speaking out.

Capitalism is good

We live in a capitalist society where we can trade freely and make as much profit as we want for ourselves with little or no restrictions on how we do this. This is the world that I live in and, without it, I would not be able to do what I do and there certainly would be no point in writing a book on how to accelerate company growth. Capitalism is a great thing and it allows countries to create wealth that ultimately trickles down to the whole of society.

Companies need to make profits; from these profits come employment and wealth for everyone. Companies need to hire and fire as appropriate to keep the business growing but as CEOs we also need to think of the wider implications for the community that we operate in when we are making commercial decisions that impact people's lives. I know that this idea of considering the social impact of our commercial decisions is an issue that many people would debate, but again many bad decisions were made in the boom times due to businesses getting greedy – for example, closing down a profitable business because the property that it operated from was worth much more than the business would ever be worth. Could the business not have been moved to cheaper premises, without the need to shut it down and put all the employees out of work?

Consider the public good

Business needs to be socially responsible to its community and the environment. For years, many businesses that operated factories totally disregarded the environment that they operated in by discharging all types of waste into fields or rivers. This caused pollution for many people who depended on this clean water for livestock or fishing – again the owners of these businesses had a total disregard for others and were only interested in maximizing profits for their own benefit.

I heard a lecture by Edward de Bono where he told the story of how one of the states in the US solved the problem of factories putting their waste into the local rivers by consulting with him to 'think' about the problem. His solution was simple: his advice was to make the factories switch their water intake pipes, which were positioned upriver taking in clean water, with their outlet pipes which were positioned downriver where they put out waste water. The switch solved the problem, because it forced the factories to use the water from the river downstream that was polluted by the factory itself. Since the factories needed clean water for their own operations, they cleaned up their act for their own benefit – and, in the process, for the benefit of the whole community.

Government's job is to make sure that decisions like this are made every day and, on the whole, it is doing a good job. But we should not wait to be told by a Government agency that what we are doing is wrong: we should have our own moral compass as a business-owner/leader and do what is right for the community while at the same time, running a profitable business. If you need to do what you know is wrong in order to make a profit, then you should not be in business in the first place.

20: Behaving Ethically in Business

Set company goals that go beyond profits

As I said earlier you need to make a profit to grow your business but, assuming you can do this, you can take your company a step further and be more successful by reaching beyond profits and engaging in Corporate Social Responsibility (CSR) . In time, CSR can generate even more profits – since it's just smart business sense.

A number of drug companies have been hugely successful by following this idea. For example, Merck developed a drug that cured river blindness, a disease that affected millions of Africans in poor countries. But after developing the drug, Merck's scientists realized that there was no profitable market for it because the people who needed it could not afford it and the governments of their countries also had no money to buy it. So the company decided to distribute the drugs free of charge to the people who needed them. Merck saved thousands of people's lives for no profit – in fact, it incurred huge losses in the process on this drug – but the overall results for the company over time were spectacular. Because of this act of kindness, their scientists were hugely motivated to see that their work went beyond profit, the general public in the developed world got to hear about their work and bought more of Merck's drugs over competitors, and over time Merck made more profits due to the decisions of their great leaders to go beyond profit.

Take a look at the humble mobile phone, which has been part of my career for many years. It is now recognized as one of the single most important developments in third world countries to help poor communities climb out of poverty. It gives them access to information, markets, health care, money transfers, etc. A good company to look at is Grameenphone, a Bangladesh mobile operator that has transformed the African landscape with its mobile phone services, that are for profit, but focused on helping poorer communities develop and grow also.

We can all do a little bit of this, or a lot if our companies are already very successful, but if you are smart about it you can use CSR to grow your profits and everyone wins in the process.

Set company values and protect your employees

The culture in an organization always depends on the leadership. So if bad behavior is tolerated in a business, then it persists and grows – sometimes it is actually initiated by the leaders.

On one of my first trips to Asia, a senior sales executive who was based there for many years explained that to do business in Asia you need to entertain guys in a different way than we do in Europe, or you won't do business in Asia at all.

I explained in return that if this was how it was done then we wouldn't be doing business in Asia. This way of entertaining may have been how things were in his world and in his time, but we have moved on and business ethics is part of every culture today. Of course, you can go down a different route and do business the old way, but you can also take a stand and insist that you only do business in an ethical way.

People who work for you expect to be treated fairly and with respect. They also expect to be safe in work and not have to worry about being bullied or taken advantage of. We cannot – must not – tolerate bullying and peer pressure in the workplace and, as leaders of growing companies, we need to make sure that everyone is respected and safe at their work. It is surprising how bullying and other inappropriate behaviors continue in the workplace today.

A senior executive of a company I know hosted a party in his house and invited a lot of younger people who reported to him. The party got out of control and the younger people were put under pressure to participate in things that they did not want to do, but many did because this person was their boss. The next day a flood of complaints came in about what had happened and the senior executive involved eventually got fired. It took some time to get this person out of the company, because of the views of the other senior managers: some wanted him fired on the spot but many simply wanted to sweep the whole affair under the carpet since the culture that already existed through the leadership had led to a level of tolerance. As leaders, we create the culture and set the tone for what is not acceptable in the workplace. It is paramount to our society that our companies are places where everyone feels safe, is valued, is treated with respect and can express themselves without fear of recrimination.

I often think of the instruction, "Do unto others as you would like them to do unto you." This works in life but it also works in business. So as a leader, do to others what you know you would like done to you, or think back on when you came up the ranks yourself and how you would like to have been treated.

It's not difficult to do but it is a question of your own values and principles as a business person. I really believe that if you exercise business ethics you and your business will be more successful in the long run than if you do not and the whole of society can benefit from your great achievement of accelerating the growth of your company.

CONCLUSION

I hope this book has helped you to accelerate the growth of your business or, at the very least, that it has made you think about different aspects of your business that could be improved. Needless to say, I don't have all the answers and this book does not attempt to give you all the answers but, based on my own experience and my experience on Accelerated Growth programs, it should cover all of the basics for you.

I started out on my own business journey with very little knowledge or experience in business. I literally made it up as I went along but, somehow, I muddled through. Each time I created a company, I learned more on the journey from start-up to accelerated growth and not all of my companies experienced growth – some crashed before we broke through the eye of the needle.

But I can safely say that I have really enjoyed my business career to date and that Digital Trading is without doubt the best company that I have ever created, with the most potential to accelerate its growth. Better still, I have been able to build it without any investors telling me what to do, so win or lose I will only have myself to thank or blame.

I cannot describe the feelings I get for my company and for business in general. I suppose you could say I am proud of what I have achieved to date; but this pride does not come from the monetary rewards. In fact, it has been less about this in latter years. In my early years, I was desperate to make money and it was a huge part of what drove me; today, I get more fulfillment from seeing my dreams become a reality: that is, investing in new products, getting them to market, getting customers to enjoy them and pay for them, then scaling the business.

I had the opportunity to speak to a class of MBS students in my old college, University College Cork. As I looked out across the lecture theatre, I remembered back to my time when I sat in those seats dreaming about being a great entrepreneur, but also worrying about how to get there. I was nobody, with no capital, no connections and little knowledge of the world outside the college gates. As I stood there in front of this class I envied them: in this new world that we live in, there are no boundaries to what we can do and what we can achieve; the only limitations are the limitations of our imaginations and our determination to make our dreams a reality. In my time, there were so many barriers to entry such as licenses to access markets, technologies that cost too much, overseas markets that cost too much to reach, communications and information systems that were too hard to use or out of reach because of costs, etc.

I told the MBS students: "There are no limits to what you can achieve today. The world is truly at your disposal. Building a technology company is like taking a blank canvas and painting the picture that you can imagine. Making your dreams a reality has never been as easy as it is today. So go dream and make them reality."

I am saying the same to you too.

Appendix 1
ACCELERATED GROWTH PLAN SLIDE DECK TEMPLATE

Below is a slide deck template for completing your own Accelerated Growth Plan. Each slide has a heading that links to a chapter in this book and, in each, I pose a number of questions that need to be answered to get to your finished slide. These are only sample questions to trigger the process and to help you get started, but they are the type of questions that are critical to any Accelerated Growth Plan. This slide deck template is available to download free of charge at **www.acceleratingcompanygrowth.com**.

COMPANY NAME
Accelerated Growth Plan
20XX – 20YY

Contents

1. Executive Summary
2. Elevator Pitch / Value Proposition
3. Market Opportunity
4. The Problem We Solve
5. How We Solve It
6. How We Sell
7. Channels to Market
8. How We Make Money
9. Competitors
10. Team to Lead This Growth
11. Finance to Fund This Growth
12. Operations to Support This Growth
13. Project Plan for Implementation
14. Core Assumptions and Key Metrics

Elevator Pitch / Value Proposition

- In one or two sentences, explain what your company does, the market it addresses and your compelling value proposition for the customer (one that's different from the competitors)
- State your vision for your company

CHAPTERS 6 & 7

Appendix 1: Accelerated Growth Plan Slide Deck Template

Market Opportunity

- What market are you addressing?
- What are the market dynamics / changes?
- What size is the market – now and future? (top-down, bottom-up research findings)
- Current / target customers and segments? (name them)
- Evidence that market opportunity exists

CHAPTER 8

The Problem We Solve

- What is the customer's problem?
- How do you solve it and where do you fit in the value chain?
- What are the benefits to the customer? (ideally stated in numbers)
- What is compelling for the target customer to buy?
- Is it big enough to make them buy? (relevant, scale, budgets, time)

CHAPTER 9

How We Solve It

- What your product does and how it works?
- What your service does? (including the service wrap)
- Who uses it and how they access it?
- Is it easy to deploy and easy to use?
- Does it change current practice, take out current suppliers, etc? (how difficult is it to sell)
- What are the unique features and benefits?
- How is it different to other solutions? (IPR, technology, innovation, insights, etc)

CHAPTER 9

How We Sell

- Market comms plans? (PR, guerrilla marketing, advertising, trade shows, speaker slots, product launches, sponsorship , digital – web, email, blog, permission marketing)
- How do you sell? Who will sell? (sales team, telesales, agents, direct, SEO)
- Length of sales cycle, outline of sales pipeline? (current pipeline to link with sales projections)
- Support materials? (presentations, brochures, demos, e-mail intro, testimonials, case study, user manual, project plans, etc)

CHAPTERS 10 & 11

Channels to Market

- Direct or indirect? (through agents, reseller partners, etc)
- Who are your partners / target partners and how can they help you scale your business?
- How do you motivate them to sell?
- How do you support them internationally?
- Why would they want to do this for you and not do it themselves?

CHAPTERS 10 & 11

How We Make Money

- What is your business model? (SaaS, product, wholesale, retail, B2B, B2C, etc)
- What is your commercial model? (once off sale, annuity, revenue share, set-up fees, consulting fees, freemium, ad funded, etc)
- Cost of sales and support? (direct costs)
- Typical revenues, costs and gross margins?
- Agent fees? (once off commission, revenue share, etc)

CHAPTER 12

Competitors

- Who are your key competitors?
- What do they do and not do compared to you?
- How could they stop you?
- Will they respond to you entering the market?
- What are the risks if they do respond?
- How will you respond to this?

CHAPTER 13

Team to Lead This Growth

- Founder / CEO? (skills, leadership style, ability to motivate, manage and lead the team, know strengths and weakness relative to team)
- Key skills required to grow the business now and future requirements? (Org Chart)
- Key skills of current team?
- What new skills do you need?
- How do you hire people with these skills?
- How do you motivate them and keep them?
- How do you manage and develop your people for growth?

CHAPTER 14

Appendix 1: Accelerated Growth Plan Slide Deck Template

Finance to Fund This Growth

- What are the finances to date? (revenues, ARPU, costs, margins, etc)
- Projected revenues and costs from future products / services? (business case, customer profiles, assumptions, sales commissions, predictability, etc)
- Capital requirements? (short and long term)
- Sources of capital and plans to bring it in as required?
- Financial risk and reward for owners / investors?
- Break even on product / service, new sales, overall business?

CHAPTER 15

3/5 Year P & L Plan

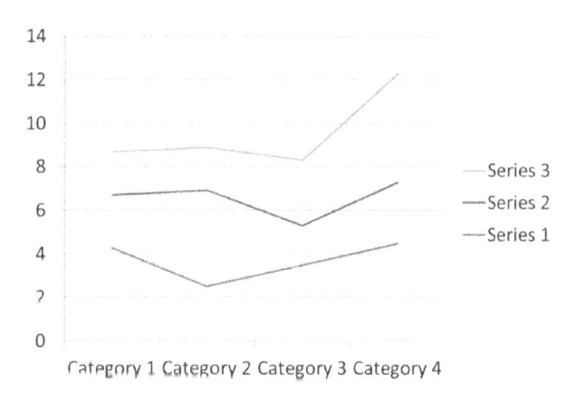

Operations to Support This Growth

- How do you support this growth?
- Product / service deployment support and control?
- Have you the buildings, staff, IT, telephones, etc to support the team and business?
- SLAs to ensure quality of service delivery to customers?
- Customer care and support back up?
- Engineering team and resources to meet demand?
- Access to raw materials on time?
- Deliveries to you and to your customer?

CHAPTER 16

Appendix 2
ACCELERATED GROWTH PLAN SAMPLE SLIDE DECK: NAUTIQUE2

This sample slide deck is based on my first company, Nautique, as if I were starting it again from scratch now. This sample slide deck is available to download free of charge at **www.acceleratingcompanygrowth.com**.

Nautique2
Dated xx/xx/xxxx

◆ Accelerated Growth Plan

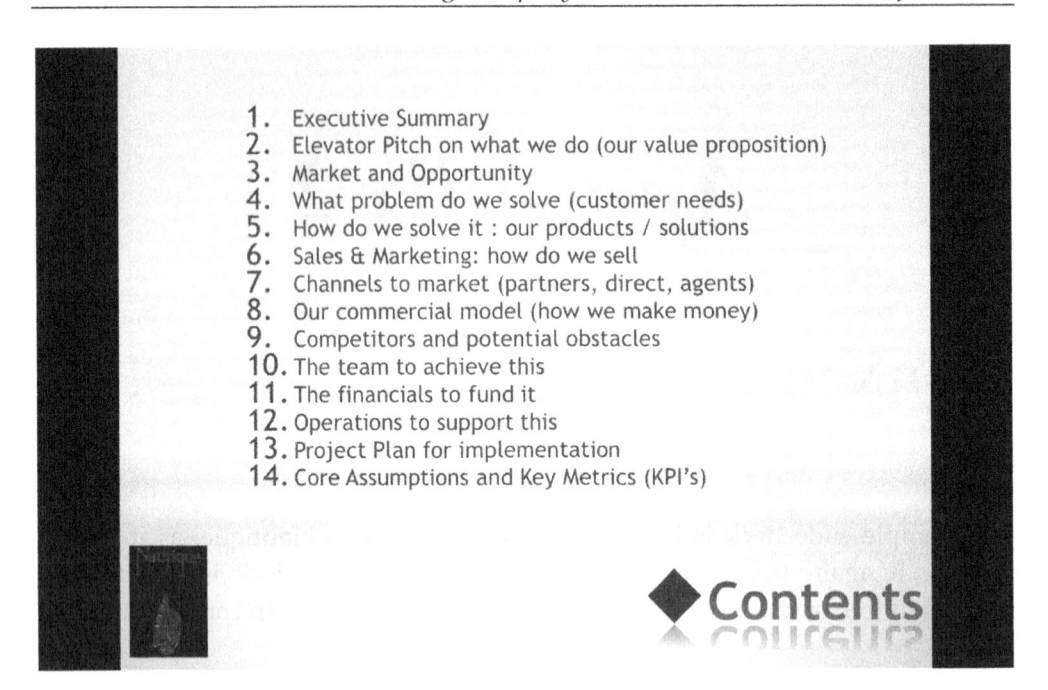

1. Executive Summary
2. Elevator Pitch on what we do (our value proposition)
3. Market and Opportunity
4. What problem do we solve (customer needs)
5. How do we solve it : our products / solutions
6. Sales & Marketing: how do we sell
7. Channels to market (partners, direct, agents)
8. Our commercial model (how we make money)
9. Competitors and potential obstacles
10. The team to achieve this
11. The financials to fund it
12. Operations to support this
13. Project Plan for implementation
14. Core Assumptions and Key Metrics (KPI's)

◆ Contents

◆ Nautique Aftershave

Appendix 2: Accelerated Growth Plan Sample Slide Deck: Nautique2

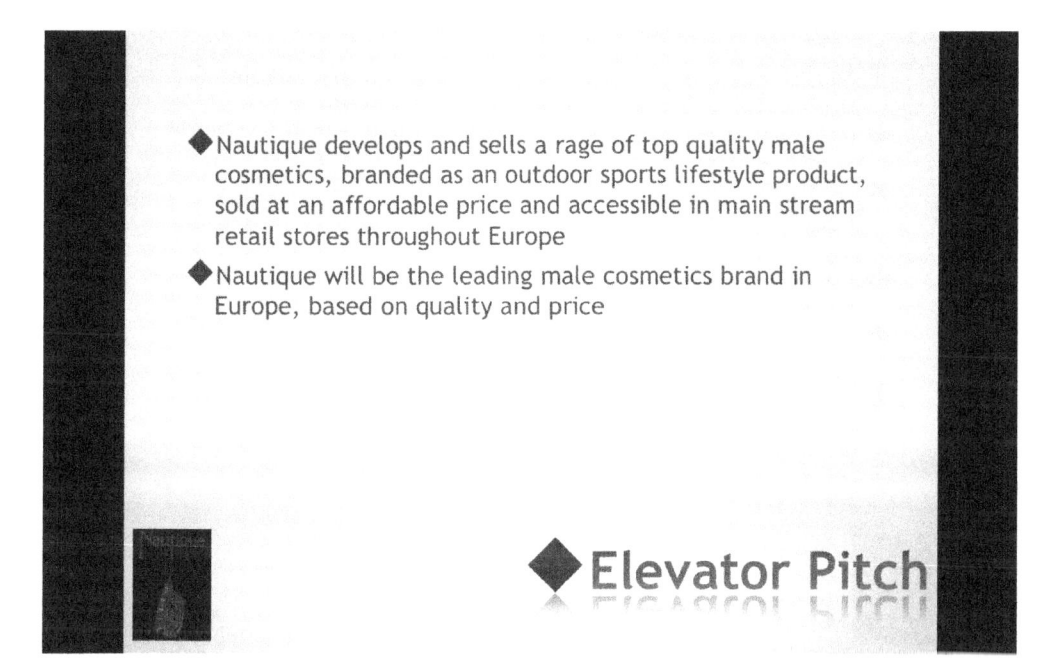

- Nautique develops and sells a rage of top quality male cosmetics, branded as an outdoor sports lifestyle product, sold at an affordable price and accessible in main stream retail stores throughout Europe
- Nautique will be the leading male cosmetics brand in Europe, based on quality and price

◆ **Elevator Pitch**

- The Global market for male cosmetics is €XX billion
  - USA €XX b, Europe €XX b, ROW €XX b
- The market is growing at a rate of XX% pa
- Top 10 brands account for xx%, non branded xx%, gap in mid market rage of branded cosmetics
- Nautique currently have XX% of Irish & UK market, based on this they expect XX% of European Market
- Sell through major grocery and Pharmacy retailers who represent XX% of all cosmetics sold using key distributors
- Sales of Nautique cosmetics increased from 0 to XXk in XXX retail store in Ireland and UK currently represent xx% of male cosmetics with three products only (aftershave, shampoo, moisturiser)

◆ **Market & Opportunity**

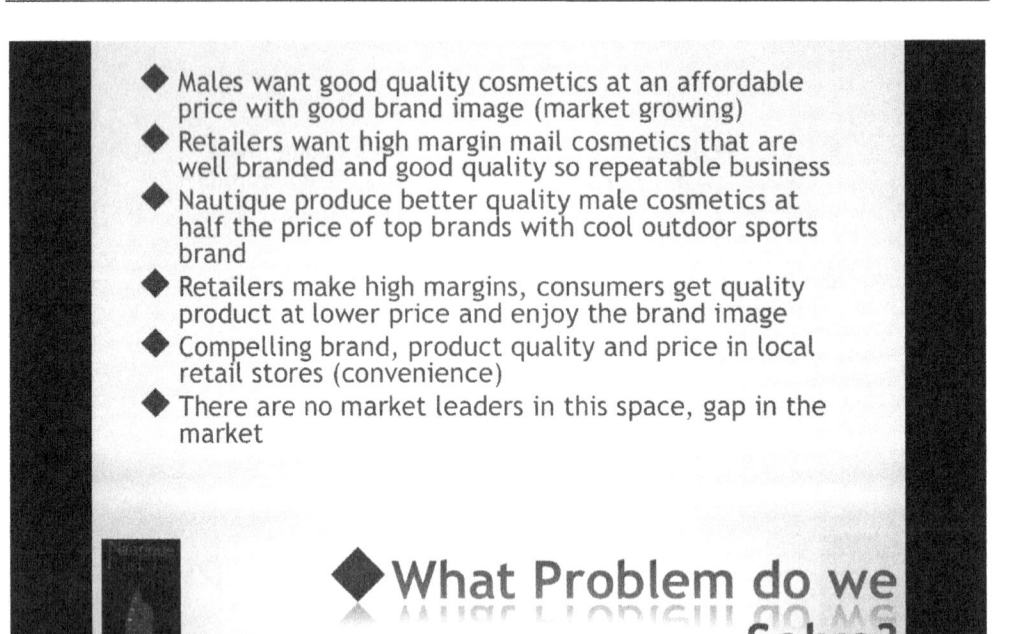

- Males want good quality cosmetics at an affordable price with good brand image (market growing)
- Retailers want high margin mail cosmetics that are well branded and good quality so repeatable business
- Nautique produce better quality male cosmetics at half the price of top brands with cool outdoor sports brand
- Retailers make high margins, consumers get quality product at lower price and enjoy the brand image
- Compelling brand, product quality and price in local retail stores (convenience)
- There are no market leaders in this space, gap in the market

◆**What Problem do we Solve?**

- Our outsource manufacturer is a leading researcher and manufacturer of cosmetics
- They can guarantee a better quality product by adding certain ingredients (e.g. more fragrance oil in aftershave)
- We are targeting males aged between 20 and 40 who play / enjoy / aspire to out doors sports,
- Products are functional to protect against weather (UV protection, moisturisers for wind etc)
- Beautiful branding, easy to use packaging for outdoor life
- Available in all major retail stores at a very low price point
- Make it cool to use Male cosmetic but encourage through outdoor protection from the weather
- No other brand has filled this gap in the market and focused on the outdoor life (cosmetic and purposeful)

◆**How do we Solve it?**

Sales & Marketing

- We distribute through major cosmetic wholesalers selling main stream cosmetics like J & J, target three in Europe (a,b,c)
- Some smaller distributors on board today that will act as references (happy with products, sell through and margins)
- Focused marketing, Point of sale promotions in store, outside store, and using demonstrators & testers (proven to work)
- High margins given to all resellers, as opposed to high profit to Nautique, to win shelf space and retailer marketing budgets
- Strong use of online marketing, blogs, social media, sports web sites using key influencers, sports stars and young outdoor leaders
- High quality point of sale branded materials, sports & sailing gear
- Market comms plans: PR, Guerrilla Marketing, Advertising
- Sponsorships of sailing clubs, sports clubs, free grear, samples
- PR around protection against skin cancer, wind burn, ageing etc

Channels to Market

- X, Y & Z Distributors reach x,xxx retailers across Europe, focused on countries a, b and c
- We focus on selling our total value proposition to cosmetic distributors, pull & push through sales to consumers
- Margins to Distributors 50%, retailers 50%
- Start in countries a, b and c, grow to x,xxx pm before entering new country
- Use local account manager for distributors
- Use in-store promotions agency for pull through
- Appoint PR agency locally, use local radio etc

Commercial Model

- 50ml Aftershave: Cost to produce €2, sell to distributor for €4, they sell to Retailer €8 retails at €16 plus VAT = €20 (other brands €40)
- Volumes per store through retailer x = 20,000 pa
- Total margin per store = €40k pa in store promotion costs = €10k pa
- Ad Agent fees on per store basis €5k
- Net margin for business = €25k
- Other products similar commercials different price points

Competitors & Obstacles

- Key competitors are top branded cosmetics (Polo, Boss, Gant, Prada)
- We offer better products at half the price
- They cannot match our prices and will not distribute through same channels
- We need top brand channels also for credibility, they could block us
- They could discredit our brand and products
- They could outspend our advertising
- They could create a new product to compete

The Team

- Great team with lots of experience in cosmetics
- Our head of R & D has worked with our outsource partners, best for R & D in this area
- Need to hire a CMO with cosmetic retail experience
- Commercial Head good contacts with key distributors
- Team have share options and 100% bonus packs
- Our vision is big the team enjoy the challenge

Finance

- We have invested over €1ml in R & D to produce 5 key products (aftershave, moisturiser, balm, shampoo & shower gel)
- Sales to date €1.5 ml Ireland, €2.5 ml UK
- No Capital requirements going forward
- All costs are variable based on sales apart from salaries
- Will bring in new VC investment at value of €10ml to accelerate sales in Europe
- Key expenditure is marketing as we deploy new distributors and retailers, cost per distributor up to €500k
- Once operational a distributor will pay back initial investment in 1 year and then contribute min €1 ml pa

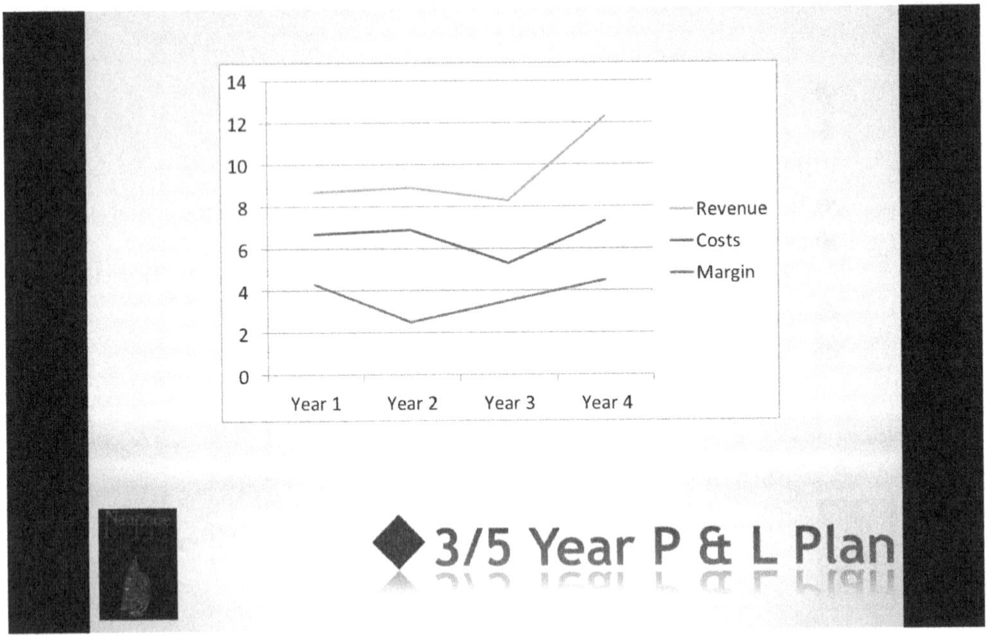
14
12
10
8
6
4
2
0
Year 1
Year 2
Year 3
Year 4
Revenue
Costs
Margin
3/5 Year P & L Plan

Senior Management all home workers
Meet once a month to coordinate strategy
We buy our unique fragrance from Grasse France (IPR)
Outsource company supply all other ingredients
Bottling and packaging supplier by outsource partner
Distributor takes order from retailers, drives production on floor of factory
We carry 10 months of stock, goods have 5 year life so can store easily, held in Outsource factory (low cost of storage)
All other operations run using Cloud services
Logistics managed by outsource company, one drop to distributor HQ so very low cost per product
Operations

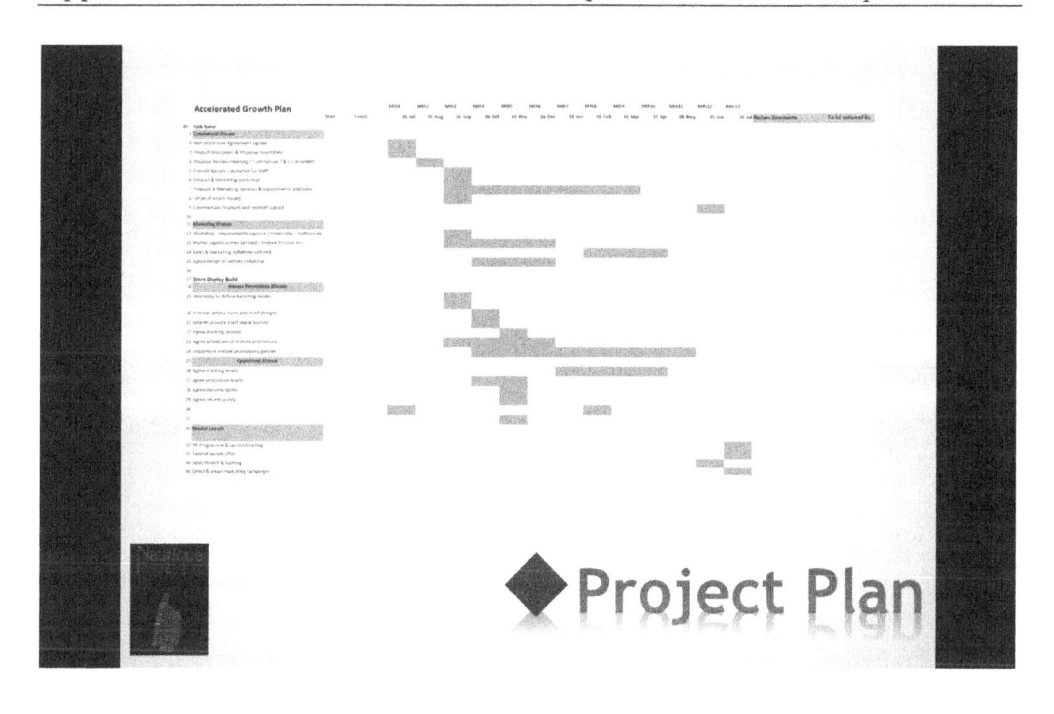

Appendix 2: Accelerated Growth Plan Sample Slide Deck: Nautique2

◆ Project Plan

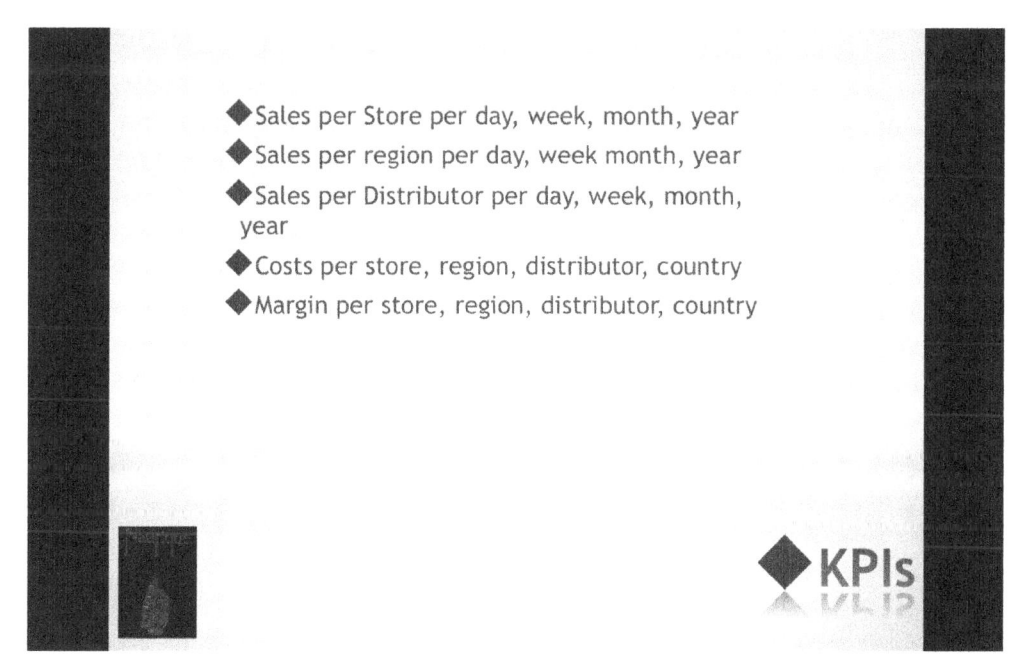

- ◆ Sales per Store per day, week, month, year
- ◆ Sales per region per day, week month, year
- ◆ Sales per Distributor per day, week, month, year
- ◆ Costs per store, region, distributor, country
- ◆ Margin per store, region, distributor, country

◆ KPIs

Appendix 3
FURTHER READING

An Unsung Hero: Tom Crean – Antarctic Survivor, Michael Smith, The Collins Press

Drive: The Surprising Truth about What Motivates Us, Daniel Pink, Canongate Books

Good to Great: Why Some Companies Make the Leap ... and Others Don't, Jim Collins, HarperBusiness

Built to Last: Successful Habits of Visionary Businesses, Jim Collins & Jerry Porras, HarperBusiness

ABOUT THE AUTHOR

Brendan Dowling is the founder and CEO of Digital Trading, a company offering cloud-based Customer Relationship Engagement (CRE) technology to governments, large and SME enterprises, through communications service providers (CSPs). He is a serial entrepreneur in the telecoms and technology sector, having built a number of successful internationally-traded companies. He also acts as a business coach with Enterprise Ireland to a number CEOs of scaling companies in the technology sector in Ireland. He is well-known for his thought leadership and innovation in the technology sector and is a regular speaker at conferences, executive education programs and government-sponsored enterprise events in Ireland, the UK and USA. Brendan qualified as a chartered accountant with KPMG, has an MBA from University College Dublin, a BComm from University College Cork (UCC) and a Diploma in Executive Coaching from IMI & UCC.

Brendan's Companies:

September 2011 – now: Executive Mentor & Coaching: Having conducted guest lectures on Entrepreneurship and Accelerating Company Growth at the IMI, Brendan was asked by the IMI to help them to design a new Accelerated Growth Program for Enterprise Ireland, in partnership with Cambridge University (Judge Business School), which is aimed at helping CEOs to accelerate the growth of their companies through thought leadership learning and one-to-one executive coaching. Brendan is an executive coach to a number of CEOs of Irish companies who are on this program. Brendan regularly gives guest lectures on business, MBA and MBS programs and at international conferences around the ICT industry. Brendan recently completed a Higher Level Diploma in Executive Coaching with the IMI / UCC.

January 2009 – now: Digital Trading Technologies Ltd, Founder and CEO: Digital Trading has designed and built a Customer

Relationship Engagement (CRE) service for communications service providers (CSPs) to sell to their enterprise customers. CRE allows enterprises to engage their customers in two-way, targeted and personalized communications *via* permission-based SMS, e-mail, letters, voice, loyalty and payments applications.

January 2008 – now: The Global Charity Platform Ltd T/A mygoodpoints.com, Founder and Chairman: mygoodpoints was developed to revolutionize the charity sector by collecting money from donors through loyalty points, payroll giving, credit cards, advertising, etc., which is then added to the donor's online wallet, where they can distribute it to charities (international and local) of their choice and receive full accountability and traceability through video feedback from the charity worker.

May 2005: iO Global Ltd, Founder and CEO: iO was a global company created by Brendan on behalf of BT after BT purchased his company, Digital Versatile Media Ltd (DVM). iO offered digital services to telecoms and media companies to allow them to sell targeted digital content and advertising over fixed and mobile networks. Customers include MTN in Nigeria, serving over 20 million subscribers, and BT in the UK; suppliers included Sony, EMI, Disney and Discovery.

January 2003: Digital Versatile Media Ltd, Founder & CEO: Brendan set up DVM to sell a full range of digital content such as video, music, newspapers, radio and games, through telcos (fixed and mobile), replicating the physical market for FMCG sales and distribution. Using hosted technology, DVM acted as a distributor for the content-owner and provided the entire technology, including end-user portals, to the telco, allowing them to brand a white label service to their own consumers. Before working with BT, DVM developed an innovative 3G portal for O2 in Ireland, which was used to show Ireland as a Digital Hub for Europe during Ireland's presidency of the EU.

August 2001: Meteor Mobile Communications Ltd, Chief Commercial Officer: Brendan worked in this role for Meteor on consultancy basis. Meteor was the third mobile network in Ireland, owned by Western Wireless International (WWI). Brendan joined when the company was eight months post-launch and significantly behind plan in its entry to the market against Vodafone and O2. He was responsible for all customer-facing activity and developed aggressive and ground-breaking strategies to turn the company around – growing the customer base from 14,000 to 1.2 million with higher than average revenues per user, before selling Meteor to eircom for a significant return on WWI's investment.

June 1996: Meridian Communications Ltd T/A imagine mobile, Founder and CEO: imagine was one of the first

MVNOs in Europe. Using a combination of simple customer-focused branding and propositions, supported by excellent customer care, telesales and direct response marketing, imagine became a success in the Irish market and was rolling out across Europe with other MNOs when it was acquired by Vodafone.

January 1994: Hire Store Limited, Owner: Brendan owned and operated a hire business in Carlow that offered DIYers and builders all types of power tools and small plant. Hire Store traded for a little more than a year and then closed.

January 1993: Dowling & Co. Chartered Accountants, Principal: Brendan owned and operated an accountancy practice that employed over 15 staff and specialized in insolvency, corporate finance and business strategy, as well as operating a traditional accountancy practice, with offices in Dublin and Carlow. He sold the practice at the height of the market and went full-time into a new telecoms venture, purchasing Meridian Communications from a former client just as the Irish market started to deregulate.

September 1991: Coopers & Lybrand, Insolvency Senior Accountant: Brendan went to London after he qualified as a chartered accountant to work in Coopers & Lybrand's corporate recovery division (Cork Gully). During his time there, Brendan managed many insolvency appointments from running the business to closing and realizing the assets for its creditors.

June 1984: Nautique Ltd, Owner: Brendan owned and operated a premium aftershave company that competed with top brands like Polo, Boss, YSL, etc. The company achieved significant growth but had to close due to litigation after it started to export to the US.

September 1987: KPMG, Trainee Chartered Accountant: Brendan trained and qualified as a chartered accountant through the Insolvency department of KPMG in Dublin. Due to his computer skills and Excel model-building expertise, Brendan also worked with the Corporate Finance department helping to develop business plans for companies looking to list on the public market and ran computer training programs for partners and senior managers within KPMG.

Other Consulting / Advisory Roles: Brendan has consulted and advised businesses in many different sectors – including technology, advertising, media, music, food, services, telecommunications, electricity, charity – to drive their innovation and to develop new strategies to help them accelerate the growth of their business or to diversify their business into new markets.

OAK TREE PRESS

Oak Tree Press develops and delivers information, advice and resources for entrepreneurs and managers. It is Ireland's leading business book publisher, with an unrivalled reputation for quality titles across business, management, HR, law, marketing and enterprise topics. NuBooks is its recently-launched imprint, publishing short, focused ebooks for busy entrepreneurs and managers.

In addition, through its founder and managing director, Brian O'Kane, Oak Tree Press occupies a unique position in start-up and small business support in Ireland through its standard-setting titles, as well as training courses, mentoring and advisory services.

Oak Tree Press is comfortable across a range of communication media – print, web and training, focusing always on the effective communication of business information.

Oak Tree Press, 19 Rutland Street, Cork, Ireland.
T: + 353 21 4313855 F: + 353 21 4313496.

E: info@oaktreepress.com

W: www.oaktreepress.com / www.SuccessStore.com.

Lightning Source UK Ltd.
Milton Keynes UK
UKOW06f1550011113

220237UK00002B/55/P

9 781781 191118